"Jeanne Mayo has lived this book. She really knows her stuff. Jeanne is energetic, enthusiastic and is absolutely in love with kids and Jesus. Her passion for and knowledge of youth ministry will inspire you on every page.

Jim Burns
President, YouthBuilders/HomeWord

"No one in the youth ministry world combines powerful insight with practical strategy better than Jeanne Mayo. Follow her sage advice in *Thriving Youth Groups* and you'll experience a youth ministry miracle—an immediate boost in both the quality of your ministry and the number of teenagers impacted by it. This is a must-have book."

Rick Lawrence
Executive Editor, GROUP Magazine

"Practical, helpful advice from someone who's been there and stayed there. This book is a must-read for anyone who's looking to build an enduring youth ministry."

Josh D. McDowell
Author/Speaker

"Jeanne Mayo's call for youth ministries to provide hospitality, a genuine welcome, sincere relationships, and a sense of belonging—and then to let Christ move the hearts of our young people—is a gentle reminder we all need to hear. She provides wonderful, real life examples and step-by-step processes for fostering effective peer ministry. This is a valuable resource!"

Robert J. McCarty
Executive Director,
National Federation for Catholic Youth Ministry

thriving
youth groups

Secrets for growing your ministry

by Jeanne Mayo

Loveland, Colorado

Group resources actually work!

This Group resource helps you focus on **"The 1 Thing™"**— a life-changing relationship with Jesus Christ. "The 1 Thing" incorporates our **R.E.A.L.** approach to ministry. It reinforces a growing friendship with Jesus, encourages long-term learning, and results in life transformation, because it's:

Relational
Learner-to-learner interaction enhances learning and builds Christian friendships.

Experiential
What learners experience through discussion and action sticks with them up to 9 times longer than what they simply hear or read.

Applicable
The aim of Christian education is to equip learners to be both hearers and doers of God's Word.

Learner-based
Learners understand and retain more when the learning process takes into consideration how they learn best.

---

thriving youth groups Secrets for growing your ministry

Copyright © 2005 Jeanne Mayo/Youth Source

All rights reserved. No part of this book may be reproduced in any manner whatsoever without prior written permission from the publisher, except where noted in the text and in the case of brief quotations embodied in critical articles and reviews. For information write Permissions, Group Publishing, Inc., Dept. PD, P.O. Box 481, Loveland, CO 80539.

Visit our Web site: www.group.com

To learn more about Jeanne Mayo's ministry, visit: www.youthsource.com

Credits
Editor: Kelli B. Trujillo

Creative Development Editor: Mikal Keefer

Chief Creative Officer: Joani Schultz

Copy Editor: Christy Fagerlin

Art Director: Jean Bruns

Designer/Illustrator: Toolbox Creative

Cover Art Director/Designer: Jeff A. Storm

Production Manager: Dodie Tipton

Unless otherwise noted, Scripture taken from the HOLY BIBLE, NEW INTERNATIONAL VERSION®. Copyright © 1973, 1978, 1984 by International Bible Society. Used by permission of Zondervan Publishing House. All rights reserved.

Library of Congress Cataloging-in-Publication Data
Mayo, Jeanne, 1949-

Thriving youth groups : secrets for growing your ministry / by Jeanne Mayo.
—1st American pbk. ed.

   p. cm.

   ISBN 0-7644-2680-X (alk. paper)

   1. Church work with youth. I. Title.

   BV4447.M352 2004

   259'.23—dc22   2004019783

10 9 8 7 6 5 4 3 2 1   14 13 12 11 10 09 08 07 06 05

Printed in the United States of America.

Contents

110647

Dedication

This book is lovingly dedicated to those who have proven to be the epicenter of my life…

To my husband, Sam, who redefines love and constancy in my life and remains my most adored hero and companion. You truly are "the wind beneath my wings."

To my eldest son, Josh, who has lived with more character and courage than any mom deserves to witness. I.L.Y.W.A.M.H.M.W.A.B.T.C.

To my "second but never last" son, Justin, who has magically merged the worlds of radical in-your-face living with radical in-your-face Christianity. Thanks for all the late-night movies and talks by the lake.

To Jordan, Lesly, Dan, Karena, Jason, Julie, Alex, Kristen, Joni, Michelle, and Carissa, who have dared to believe in the dream of Youth Source and have consistently made such selfless investments of their brilliance and energy.

To Ken, Kathy, and Barbara, who remain treasured friends whose prayers and sacrifices made this whole ministry dream of mentoring youth pastors possible.

To the youth ministry dream teams I've loved from Rockford, Bellevue, and Sacramento, who always gave me the "why behind the what."

To the emerging team in Atlanta (especially Darren, Jordan, and Matt), who remind me daily why youth ministry has captured the essence of my lifelong passion, heart, and mission.

And to the thousands of breathtaking youth leaders and teenagers along the journey, who have allowed me the priceless honor of being "Jesus with skin on" in their lives.

Together we celebrate the reality of our relentless Savior who sends us out to pursue today's youth culture with his relentless love.

Acknowledgments

Friends in your life are like pillars on your porch: Sometimes they hold you up; sometimes they lean on you; sometimes it's just enough to know they're standing by.

I'd like to express my most sincere thanks to a few of the individuals who have been such great friends and "pillars" to me through the process of writing this book.

To my treasured "pillar," Lesley Butcher, whose brilliance was only outshined by her tenacious love and loyalty. I am unworthy of your talent, your heart, and your untold hours of diligence. Lesley, Jesus and I are both clapping very loudly for you.

To my new "pillar," Kelli Trujillo, whose role as my editor and cheerleader broke all my previous stereotypes and created an exciting new mental paradigm for book editors. Thank you for always making me feel so deeply heard.

To two of youth ministry's most historic "pillars," Thom and Joani Schultz, the founder and owners of Group Publishing, who dared to take a chance on a youth ministry veteran they had never even met named Jeanne.

And to one final "pillar" named Rick Lawrence, whose encouragement during a chance meeting on our way to Newfoundland rewrote personal history for me. Your integrity and trustworthiness make your words very loud in my life, Rick. Thank you for saying that day, "Jeanne, you have youth ministry years inside of you that need to be chronicled." Late that night when you slipped back to your seat on the airplane, Jesus and I had a long talk. Thank you, my friend. I was listening.

Introduction

Vince Lombardi once said that "any man's finest hour…is that moment when he has worked his heart out in a good cause and lies exhausted on the field of battle—victorious." So as I write these words to you, I find myself looking for a field to fall down in. At last, *Thriving Youth Groups: Secrets for Growing Your Ministry* is completed. It is my privilege to address you personally in these opening pages. And then I will write a mental, "It is finished" over this long-awaited project.

How do I end (and begin) something that is such an integral part of my DNA? I want to begin by saying a sincere thank you for picking up this book. But at the risk of sounding cheesy, allow me to share my heart with you. After nearly thirty-five years in full-time youth ministry, I know how agonizing and lonely the journey can become. I've met face to face with literally thousands of amazing youth leaders through the years, many marked by a sense of failure and futility. The most commonly asked question through my journey has been, "What did you do to make this youth group grow so much and still radiate spiritual vitality?"

Thriving Youth Groups: Secrets for Growing Your Ministry contains the key principles from my youth ministry journey. Most of these growth concepts center around creating a friendship culture where teenagers feel an authentic sense of affirmation and belonging. In each chapter, I've tried to show you the strategic steps we have taken, time after time, to create an atmosphere of Christ-honoring love where students want not only to come back, but also to bring their friends. I've also included some thoughts and ideas that have been shared with me by youth leaders around the country; I hope their practical insights are helpful to you as you work to make your ministry thrive.

I'm a pragmatic individual at heart. So while I've attempted to tell you key stories that have punctuated my journey, I've remained heavy on the "how to's." Like you, I know the discouragement of giving youth ministry your best and still dealing with low attendance, cliques, and utter lack of interest among the students. Throughout the book, I've tried to systematically demystify the whole process of creating a welcoming, growing youth ministry.

It's really no surprise to most of us who have been in youth ministry for a while: The number one thing teenagers want in a youth ministry is a relational, welcoming environment. But how do you create and sustain that kind of atmosphere in the self-centered, insecure youth culture we now minister to? That's what I've tried to chronicle in the following chapters.

So go grab a cup of your favorite java, find a comfortable chair, and let's begin to travel the "youth ministry trail" together. I've made so many mistakes that hopefully my vulnerability will save you a few mishaps of your own. You see, you as a youth leader are really the "big deal" of my spiritual journey now. Though I am continuing in local youth ministry just like you, my primary life mission now is "to encourage, equip, inspire, and instruct the youth leaders of this generation."

Thank you for allowing me to be somewhat of a "big sis" in the youth ministry trenches. I've never known anyone who made it to the Olympics without a coach, and so I pray that this book will allow me to be a long-distance coach and mentor to you, even if we never get to meet this side of heaven.

Let me close by sharing the words that have often inspired me to go the long haul in youth ministry, no matter how costly or demanding the journey. They are the words of the historic missionary Jim Elliot: "He is no fool who gives what he cannot keep to gain what he cannot lose." That's a pretty great anthem for those of us in youth ministry; don't you think?

Lovingly Honored to Be in Your Life,
Jeanne

P.S. I checked in with Jesus this morning. He wanted me to remind you that he's grateful for all your sacrifices in youth ministry, and he's pretty crazy about you...for real.

{Unashamedly, I am a frog kisser.}

Chapter 1

Welcome to the World of Frog Kissing

"People have a way of becoming what you encourage them to be."—John Mason

I have a confession to make. Unashamedly, I am a frog kisser. Yes, you heard it right. I, Jeanne Mayo, am (and have been for several decades) a proud card-carrying member of Youth Ministry Frog Kissers of America. As a matter of fact, my frog kissing obsession has probably been the key to my significance in youth ministry. Don't worry; I'll explain. It was an unforgettable youth night several years ago that launched me into this preoccupation with frog kissing. Allow me to relive it with you.

We had worked intensely to create an incredible youth night—trust me; it was destined to be a success. We built the entire evening around a relevant theme. We used various creative communication techniques, and we'd packed the place with hundreds of excited, screaming teenagers. Most importantly, we had prayed our guts out that the evening would make Jesus smile. When I gave the students an opportunity to respond to Christ at the conclusion of the service, the reaction was staggering. It was no Billy Graham service, but enough to be remembered as an unforgettable night in my mind.

Then it happened—without warning, the picture-perfect youth night came to a screeching halt. As I slipped to the back of our meeting room to give high fives to a couple of our key leaders who had worked especially hard, I overheard a conversation that served as a painful wake-up call. Apparently, a parent was picking up her teenager at the conclusion of the service. I heard the mom casually ask her son, "What'd you think?" The teenager took less than a second to formulate his direct four-word reply: "I'm not coming back!"

I picked my heart up off the floor, and I took off after the teenage guy before he could walk out the door. "Look, my name is Jeanne," I said, trying to get his attention. "I did some of the talking up front tonight. What's your name?"

In a direct voice, the high school guy spouted off his first name and then turned to walk away. (We'll call him "Ben" to protect the innocent.) I was not willing to be ditched so easily, so I followed him closer to the door.

"Look, Ben," I said, feeling slightly embarrassed. "I was standing in the back of the room a few minutes ago and overheard your comments to your mom. I heard you tell her you weren't coming back." His eyes flashed defensively for a second as if he were gearing up for a debate. But I continued. "Would you help us out by telling me where we bombed tonight? I mean, a sharp guy like you would be a huge asset around here. Please tell me what'd we do wrong?"

Ben's eyes softened a little, and he paused for a second before answering. "It wasn't what people *did* that was the turnoff. It was what they *didn't* do."

"OK, now you've really got me curious. What did we *not* do?" I asked. It was becoming obvious to me that Ben wasn't a socially needy kid. He came across like a sharp, put-together high school guy, but whatever had occurred that night in our youth meeting had obviously created a stingingly negative impression.

> ## God Makes It Good!
>
> "I had some local high school students who started coming around because I asked them to play basketball with me. From there I asked them to visit our student ministry on Wednesday night. They showed up and have hardly missed a service since. Recently I discovered that some of them have been kicked out of school, been rejected by their parents, or have been in and out of juvenile hall. I talked to them about receiving Jesus Christ, and one responded, 'God doesn't want me—I am wasted goods.' I was able to tell them that God takes what we think is wasted and makes it good. That's what frog kissing is all about!"
>
> —Todd Bishop, a youth pastor in Valley Stream, New York

"Our service or program may be great, but if teenagers don't feel friendliness or acceptance by their peers, they're not coming back."

"I'll tell you what you *didn't* do. My mom conned me into coming, and nobody acted like they gave a rip if I was here. *Nobody* talked to me, like I was invisible or something. I'd rather spend my time with people who at least *pretend* like they're glad I showed up. That's why I won't be coming back anymore."

I attempted to do damage control with Ben as he headed out the door, but his body language made it clear that he was through talking. As the glass door to the youth room shut abruptly behind him, I became painfully aware that our unfriendliness had probably closed some doors in his heart, doors that needed to be open before there could be an authentic faith commitment. We had blown it. Amidst our great music, inspiring message, and great drama that night, we had failed to focus on the one thing that matters most in today's youth culture: an atmosphere of authentic friendship.

Ben's abrupt answer sliced through my youth ministry euphoria that night like a knife. But as cutting as his reply was, I've discovered it should not have been surprising. An article published in Group Magazine revealed the results of their "Cool Church" survey, which involved approximately ten thousand Christian teenagers. In the survey, teenagers were asked to rate ten different factors that influence their commitment to church on a sliding scale from "not at all important" to "very important." The highest ratings in the "very important" category were the following:

#1—A welcoming atmosphere where you can be yourself—73 percent.

#2—Quality relationships with other teenagers—70 percent.

Interestingly enough, the response that came in dead last at 21 percent was:

#10—A fast-paced, high-tech, entertaining ministry approach.

I remember walking back into the youth area that night feeling like a failure. What I thought had been a ministry "home run" suddenly appeared more like a "strikeout" in the eyes of some of our attendees. So what's the bottom line? Our *service or program* may be great, but if teenagers don't feel friendliness or acceptance by their peers, they're not coming back. Youth leader Steve Miller, in the Group Magazine article "The Secrets of Welcoming Youth Groups," warns: "If your group fails the friendliness test, visitors will never return." He encourages all of his student leaders to assume that all newcomers visiting their ministry "are making a last-ditch effort to find someone who cares about them before they end it all."

So what does all of this have to do with frog kissing? Everything. You see, I've been in full-time youth ministry (full-time frog kissing) for three and a half decades. I laughingly tell my audiences at leadership conferences that I've been in youth ministry so long that I can remember when the Dead Sea was still sick! But before you rule me out because I'm too dated to still have a relevant voice in 21st century youth ministry, let me give you a brief overview of my journey. I directed a youth ministry in Nebraska that grew from zero to 350 students who were meeting on a weekly basis. Then I went to Illinois where we saw growth from thirty-five students to approximately one thousand each week. Years later in my career, the Lord allowed me to "suffer for his sake" in sunny California. People told me when we first arrived that "Youth ministry will be harder on the West Coast. Teenagers aren't the same there." But after approximately one year in Sacramento, the weekly participation grew from about eighty students to well over five hundred.

As I write this book, the same kind of exciting turnaround is happening in Atlanta where we've renamed the youth outreach "Oxygen." Why do I tell you all of that? No, I'm not trying to convince you that youth ministry significance is all about numbers—it isn't. But without apology, I must say that I am convinced Christ didn't give his life on a cross so that we could minister to empty chairs. We can't spiritually impact students who are never around us. You don't need to have graduate degrees in theology to recognize that making a difference in God's kingdom requires us to go after people.

What's the Bottom Line in Youth Ministry Growth?

Through my exciting years in youth ministry, many sincere youth leaders have come to visit our various youth ministries. And all of these extraordinary people had one bottom-line question: "How did the growth occur?

Jeanne, what's the secret?" They usually expect me to give them some magic formula we've implemented in our programming or in our leadership structure. Other well-meaning people quietly drop their voices and ask, "Jeanne, how many hours do you pray each day?" But through the years, my consistent answer has been both surprising and a little disappointing for many of them. I tell them that we're into frog kissing, and because of that, one of our key goals is to become one of the friendliest places in the city. Have we made it yet? Not hardly. But every Wednesday evening when teenagers walk into the door, we ask God to help us make Christ-honoring friendliness the point of our spear. It's the principle of the old theme song from the sitcom *Cheers*. I'm convinced that the writer must have been in youth ministry because the truth is we all do want to be where everybody knows our name.

Remember the Old Fairy Tale?

Getting back to my opening confession: I, Jeanne Mayo, am a charter member of Youth Ministry Frog Kissers of America, and this book is my unashamed attempt to recruit you to join up as well. This all stems from a fairy tale you probably heard as a child. The impact of its message has become my mantra over the past thirty-five years in youth ministry.

Once upon a time, there was a handsome prince who lived far, far away. He was so handsome that all the fair maidens of the village fell madly in love with him—even the old ugly witch. One day, the witch could no longer contain herself, and she began to hit on the handsome prince. But as you might expect, the fairy tale prince wasn't too impressed. He grew so irritated with her repeated advances that he shunned her in no uncertain terms. And can you blame him? Imagine being hit on by a witch.

The ugly old witch at first was devastated. Then she became angry...very angry. "No handsome prince is going to get away with this!" she said to herself. "I'll show that young punk a thing or two. I'll cast an evil spell on him, and from this day forward, he'll no longer be a handsome prince. Oh, no, from this day forward, he'll be an ugly little frog!"

The wicked witch laughed to herself as she finished concocting the evil spell by adding one final clause—the spell could never,

ever be broken…*unless* the ugly little frog was *kissed by a beautiful princess!* Impossible odds, wouldn't you say? Even the homely guys in your youth group would have had a better chance of getting a beautiful princess to kiss them than an ugly little frog.

And with her declaration, the evil witch waves her wand and with a "Wish! Bam! Boom!" she casts the agonizing spell on our beloved prince. Not realizing what's going on, he finds himself transformed into the body of an ugly, slime-covered, warty little frog. Alone and ashamed, he spends countless hours, day after day, trapped inside this cruel masquerade. He sits on a lily pad crying out, "I'm not an ugly frog. I'm really a handsome prince. Can't anyone see past my ugly warts on the outside to see who I really am? How am I ever going to get a beautiful princess to break this spell by kissing me?"

Years passed because, after all, beautiful princesses just don't kiss ugly frogs. But one day the impossible happened. A beautiful princess came walking by the pond where the little frog had settled. He could smell her perfume in the distance, and he knew that it would be his only chance at recapturing his true destiny. As the princess drew closer, he began to utter his most seductive "Croak… croak." Strangely enough, she felt drawn to the little wart-covered frog. As she stood gazing over him in the pond, he looked up and mustered one final provocative "Croak!"

Then it happened. Emotion overtook the beautiful princess, and in a weak moment, she picked up the pitiful looking frog, looked him squarely in the eyes, and planted a royal kiss right on top of his warts! The little frog began to shake uncontrollably, and with a "Wish! Bam! Boom!" the demoralizing spell was forever broken. The kiss of the beautiful princess, who was able to look past his ugly warts, restored him to his one true destiny—that of a handsome prince.

What's that got to do with creating a welcoming, friendly youth ministry? *Everything.* You see, today's youth culture is filled with "handsome

> **❝**You choose to look past the warty junk on the outside and discover the incredible things that are always—**always**—somewhere hidden on the inside.**❞**

princes" who have had a million different things cast a spell on them. When they come to your youth ministry, most of them look pretty "froggy." They show warts of apathy, cynicism, and rebellion that many times turn away even the most seasoned youth leaders. But I hope as you read this book you'll realize that in order to create a friendly, welcoming youth ministry, you're going to have to train yourself to look past their froggish warts and see the royalty that Christ has put inside each one of them. What's the kiss? The magical transformation in your teenagers will come after you, your adult leaders, or your students, in the name of Christ's love, offer them the kiss of encouragement. You choose to look past the warty junk on the outside and discover the incredible things that are always—*always*—somewhere hidden on the inside.

Go Where They Are

"One thing we have learned in the inner city is teenagers don't just want to hear how much you care. They want to see how much you care. We are so much more effective when we go down to their neighborhoods. When we stopped expecting it to be their job to come see us and got into their neck of the woods, our chances of reaching them grew much bigger. They're looking for someone who won't give up on them—who is willing to believe in them and go the extra mile to know you are not just talk—you actually care."

—Stella VanGerwen, youth pastor in urban Los Angeles, California

Sound too childish or irrelevant? The greatest "youth minister" in the world, Jesus Christ himself, was a proud frog kisser. Remember when he was attempting to lead his twelve-man leadership team, the disciples? There was a "warty one" named Simon. Simon had a lot of potential, and Jesus knew it. He was great in front of people and always a crowd favorite, but apparently Simon had some of the same issues your potential leaders may have. He was always opening his mouth and sticking his foot in it. He made all sorts of promises that he never followed through on, and one night he got so violent he cut a guy's ear off. That probably would have been excusable, considering the circumstances; but when Christ needed his disciples most, Simon denied that he *even knew Jesus*. The New Testament account from Luke 22 tells us that he wimped out, cursed, and denied he had anything to do with the Messiah. Stop and take a moment to tell yourself, "Hey, at least my leaders haven't cut off any ears or denied they know me. I'm not doing so bad."

What Was Christ's Response to Simon the Frog?

Christ's response to Simon's froggish conduct was something a little unexpected. *Jesus changed his name.* He believed in Peter. In Matthew 16 Jesus announced to Simon that his name was now going to be Peter, which means *rock*. Peter was no longer an average little pebble—Jesus called him to be a big boulder. Jesus was sending Simon Peter a life-changing signal that day by saying, "Take heart, Pete. I'm looking past the froggish impression of your little pebble nature. I'm not going to write you off simply because of what I see on the outside. I see you as the big boulder that my Father has made you to be. You have a future, a purpose, and a destiny, Peter. I'm choosing to believe in you consistently and authentically, and I know we're going to uncover it."

Did Peter change instantly and quit being froggy? No...and neither will your teenagers change immediately. It's a process.

Maybe you've picked up this book because you want to change the friendliness quotient in your youth ministry? Maybe you want it to become a place where guests visit and want to return? Maybe you want to see cliques and social barriers broken among your teenagers? Maybe you're reading because you just want to see your group grow? Before you jump to the next chapter, prayerfully ask the Lord to enroll you in Frog Kissing 101.

Remember Ben, the guy who gave me *my* brutal wake-up call? I know that soon all the Bens in your life will be forever grateful that you took the time to read this book—and more importantly, applied it. If you want to lower the "I'm not coming back" factor, remember that we teach what we know, but we reproduce who we are. Your youth ministry will never be more genuinely friendly than you are. It's time to zero in on a couple of "croaking teenagers" and start kissing frogs!

> **We teach what we know,
> but we reproduce who we are.**

Now What? Ideas

Use these ideas to put the principles
in this chapter into action:

- Study some of Jesus' frog kissing and the impact his love and kindness had on the lives of people like Peter (Matthew 16:13-19 and Acts 2:14-41), Paul (Acts 8:1; 9:1-31), Zacchaeus (Luke 19:1-10), the Samaritan woman (John 4:1-42), Thomas (John 20:24-31), and the thief on the cross (Luke 23:36-43).

- Find a picture of yourself as a young teenager. Remember the awkwardness and insecurity of adolescence. What were your warts? How did you feel froggish? Put the picture in your wallet or purse as a reminder to see the real person behind a teenager's froggish behavior.

- Pick an upcoming evening, and ask a couple of your more perceptive students to experience your youth service through the eyes of a newcomer. Have them report back to you on their findings.

- Take some time to reflect on at least one person who saw past your "warts" and helped you become who you are today through their frog kissing in your life. Think about the simple but effective things this person did to give you "the kiss of encouragement."

- Make a list of students whom you personally helped to become a "prince" or "princess" in the last year through your authentic friendliness and belief+ in them.

- Make a list of some current students you are targeting, who are still "pretty warty."

- On a scale of one to ten, rate yourself on how well you are doing in the area of intentional friendship and warmth.

_____

_____

_____

_____

_____

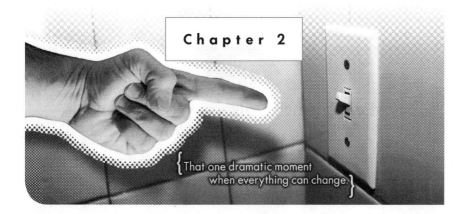

{That one dramatic moment when everything can change.}

Seven Steps to Immediately Change Everything

Malcolm Gladwell defines a "tipping point" as "that one dramatic moment in an epidemic when everything can change all at once." Though it's not written from a spiritual viewpoint, Gladwell's groundbreaking best seller, *The Tipping Point,* holds powerful implications for your youth ministry journey, providing a model for how you can quickly develop an "epidemic" of friendship and warmth in your group. Gladwell's premise is that little changes can create remarkably big differences. In *The Tipping Point,* Gladwell points out three characteristics of an epidemic: its ability to be contagious, its ability to result in big effects from little causes, and its ability to create drastic change in one extraordinary moment.

These characteristics are seen in the way a flu epidemic moves through a classroom or how a new style of music suddenly becomes the rage in popular culture. Let's take it a step further: These same principles can help you create an *epidemic of friendliness and numerical growth* in your own youth ministry. In the following pages, you'll find seven practical steps you can take right away that will result in dramatic change in your youth ministry culture and ultimately will help you create your own ministry tipping point.

Caution: These steps may not be profound, but I guarantee they will be effective. How do I know? I've followed the same pattern in all four youth ministries I've led in the past thirty-five years and experienced results of epidemic proportion.

Step 1

Pull together a diverse group of key students and say, "Talk to me."

Ministry is probably the only significant 21st century "business" that doesn't regularly host focus groups to determine the level of "customer satisfaction." Yet this type of feedback is *essential* if you want students to feel valued! Conducting informal feedback groups will help you get the pulse of the "perceived reality" of your students.

I often find that teenagers' perception of reality is surprisingly different than my own. If you want to create a friendship tipping point in your youth ministry, host a strategic feedback meeting to help you get started. Here are a few guidelines for your own meeting:

- Select key students from different age groups and with different social statuses.

- Choose students who are outgoing enough to honestly give you their own opinions.

- Make sure the students at least occasionally participate in your youth ministry.

- Invite about one-tenth to one-fifth of your group's normal number of participants. (So, for example, if your group has thirty teenagers, you'll want to invite three to six students to your meeting.)

- Send out letters or private invitations so participants feel they're being invited to something special.

- Let invitees know that you need their help to strategically chart the future of the youth ministry. Set the time, make it convenient, and host it away from the church building if possible.

• To ensure that they all show up, call and remind them about the meeting a few days ahead of time.

A few years ago, when we launched our exciting turnaround in Sacramento, I hosted my own Talk to Me meeting. The youth ministry I inherited had two primary reputations among the students who had stopped attending:

Reputation #1—It was boring.

Reputation #2—It was really *unfriendly.*

The "really" was always emphasized when kids said it. One teenager even added, "I visited not long ago and felt like Osama bin Laden at a church picnic!" That's pretty bad.

I felt we could handle the "boring" issue by making a few simple pragmatic changes to the weekly meetings; but the tougher and more strategic transition was going to be changing the "*really* unfriendly," "Osama bin Laden" part. The core students who regularly attended the youth ministry at that time were good kids, not at all purposefully unfriendly. But as a result of long-running social circles, insecurity, and a lack of motivation, they'd become pretty self-absorbed. The previous leaders had been fine, Christ-honoring individuals who modeled authentic friendship to the teenagers; they just fell a little short when it came to getting the overall friendship tenor of the youth ministry to make a dramatic change. In Gladwell's terms, they didn't know how to create a friendship tipping point.

The agenda at our Talk to Me meeting was pretty simple. I shared from my heart with the teenagers that we wanted to begin "chapter two" in the life of our ministry and that it should be punctuated by a genuine atmosphere of friendship and warmth. I reiterated how much I needed their help and explained that I had four questions I wanted their input on. My words that night went something like…

"With the Lord's help, we want to become one of the friendliest places a teenager can come to on a Wednesday night in Sacramento. We want to be the kind of place that you're proud to invite your nonchurched friends to. So talk to me about a few things…"

Question #1: "I think we'd all agree that we can improve on the friendliness factor. What are some of the things that happen in our youth meetings that give off a feeling of unfriendliness?"

"Those teenagers are your 'customers'—their input is critical in your efforts to create a thriving and growing youth ministry."

The discussion took awhile to get going, but I waited, nodded my head, and took notes. They slowly but surely got the idea that I was genuinely interested in all of their comments. I was careful not to get defensive or react. I just listened and "primed the pump" occasionally by phrases like, "That's really good! Somebody else talk to me."

Question #2: "What simple things could we do or change that would improve our friendliness factor on Wednesday nights?"

When the first couple of suggestions were met with a sincere, "That's a good idea," the floodgates opened up. Among their comments were lines like, "You're an OK speaker, but we like it when you don't talk for such a long time." They made me take a look at some of the lyrics to the songs we sang, saying their friends would never "get them."

Question #3: "What are we already doing in our youth ministry that you like? things that we want to be sure to hold onto?"

Don't be heartbroken if these answers come pretty slowly. Today's youth culture has learned to be naturally critical but not naturally encouraging.

Question #4: "What would need to change in our weekly youth ministry gathering to make it the kind of place you would feel comfortable asking your nonchurched friends to attend? Nothing you say is going to come across wrong or disrespectful. I need honest feedback. What are some things that might need to change?"

Again, I listened, nodded, and wrote.

When they were done, I expressed my thanks and held up the yellow legal pad of notes as a reminder that I took their suggestions seriously. I let them know that approximately one month from that time, we would be hosting a relaunch of the youth ministry, a youth night we'd call Chapter 2. I promised them we'd work to implement several of their suggestions. Most of all, I asked them for their help and prayers on changing the atmosphere of the group. I shared with them one of my favorite sayings: "Friendship is the paved highway the Holy Spirit most often travels on."

We closed in prayer and asked Jesus to initiate a Chapter 2 era in the life of our youth ministry—one of authentic friendship and love.

The next week, I took about eight minutes during our regular youth meeting to have everyone complete an anonymous survey using the same four questions outlined above. After gathering all of that feedback, I used it to make plans for changes, and I read several of their answers aloud in upcoming youth meetings.

This first step of going behind the scenes to ask questions of your students may seem unimportant, but the truth is that those teenagers are your "customers"—their input is critical in your efforts to create a thriving and growing youth ministry.

Step 2

Create an S.I.P. with target Velcro points.

In my world, S.I.P. stands for "System in Place." In this step, you go beyond just analyzing, collecting information, and dreaming; and start writing down a specific plan of attack. I suggest you formulate this written strategy with the help of a few key players (either student or adult leaders) and work to include the ideas you got from students in your Talk to Me meeting. Also, make sure your S.I.P. focuses specifically on "Velcro points." In other words, work with your team to identify actions that will provide greater "stickiness" for guests and fringe students, helping them connect with and attach to your group. Your S.I.P. plan should identify specific and measurable goals assigned to people and include deadlines for accomplishing those goals. Without this step, your good intentions will remain just that: merely good intentions.

Here's a skeleton of the S.I.P. we created when we relaunched the youth ministry in Sacramento. There's no magic in what we wrote down, but it can serve as a guide as you create your own S.I.P. When we launched our S.I.P., we also renamed the youth outreach meetings "Oxygen" with the tag line "Come up for air!" By changing the name of the youth meetings, we were able to communicate that we were totally committed to starting a new era.

Oxygen's S.I.P. Plan

Launch Date: October 6

Action	People in Charge	Deadline
Select 8 students to be door greeters.	Chris and Katherine	Sunday, September 5
Host 1-hour training for greeters.	Chris and Katherine	Sunday, September 12
Create guest registration card.	Kyle	Monday, September 13
Make 300 copies of guest registration card.	Kyle	Tuesday, September 14
Make a list of influencers we want to invite to a Paul Revere meeting.	Jeanne and Josh	Sunday, September 5
Write a letter and make calls to all those on the Paul Revere list.	Tiffany	Tuesday, September 7
Talk privately to Jessica and Mackenzie about positively influencing all the sophomores to get more involved.	Katie and Sarah	Tuesday, September 7
Brainstorm ideas for holding a guest reception.	Jon, Nate, Aaron, and Heather	Wednesday, September 8
Outline key points that need to be on the video to be shown during the guest reception, schedule time to record staff and key students, present to Jeanne for suggestions.	Jon, Nate, Aaron, and Heather	Wednesday, September 22
Put together presentation to show William's dad, Chris' parents, and Mary's grandma about underwriting our new launch and providing $200 to help purchase a Ping Pong table and foosball table for the group.	Jeanne, Heidi, and Mark	Sunday, September 19
Plan the content of the Paul Revere meeting.	Jeanne	Sunday, September 12
Enlist Anne and Justin to write a 5-minute skit for the Chapter 2 night on how **not** to treat visitors at Oxygen.	Paula and Jordan	Sunday, September 12
Finalize edits on guest reception video.	Jon and Nate	Sunday, September 26
Ask Morgan, Brandon, and Steve to share personally at the Chapter 2 night about needing friendships.	Jeanne	Monday, September 20
Host a Paul Revere meeting and provide each attendee with 5 to 10 names of students to personally invite to the Chapter 2 night.	Jeanne, Paula, and Alicia	Sunday, October 3
Launch Greeter Team, Greeter Table, Name Tags, Guest Reception, Hang Out Areas.	The whole gang	Wednesday, October 6
Host Chapter 2 night.	The whole gang	Wednesday, October 6

Step 3

Host a Paul Revere meeting for key influencers.

On the evening of April 18, 1775, Joseph Warren became convinced that the British army was about to march against Lexington and Concord. The events that unfolded right after this were reinterpreted in a poem penned by Longfellow, which became the popular legend of "Paul Revere's Ride."

In the popular—if historically questionable—version of events, Warren wanted the local militia alerted so they'd be ready for the British. He sent out Paul Revere and William Dawes to pass along word of the impending attack.

Revere's famous ride had monumental results. For two hours he rode through the night, notifying civic leaders of the attack so they, in turn could alert others. Sleeping towns sprang to life with bells ringing and citizen soldiers readying themselves for battle. When the British arrived, they found readied American troops. The British were defeated, and the American Revolution launched.

William Dawes' efforts to alert his countrymen, on the other hand, did *not* become the stuff of legend. Like Revere, Dawes was captured and released by the British. Like Revere, he rode to alert militia leaders, and he carried urgent news. Yet, Dawes' name has faded from view while Revere remains a folk hero.

Why?

According to some, Revere was enormously effective at finding the right people to notify. He banged on the doors of key influencers, while Dawes was less successful connecting with citizens who could alert local troops.

The result: Revere's message prompted action, while Dawes' message was in part ignored or misunderstood.

The third step you'll want to take is to hold a "Paul Revere" meeting to give influential students the scoop on the changes that will be taking place

> *"Authentic friendship is necessary in communicating the message of Christ."*

in your group. Be sure to invite all the teenagers from your Talk to Me session as well as a much broader base of students—the more, the merrier. A good number to invite is about 50 percent of your overall weekly attendance. Also be sure to include several fringe students who may not currently be attending or who only visit sporadically.

I started our Paul Revere meeting by sharing the story of Revere and Dawes and then went on to say...

> So why did I ask you to show up tonight? I guess I want you to know that I view each of you as Paul Reveres in a world full of William Dawes. You have the ability to influence the people around you. I'm asking you to use that influence to create a revolution of authentic friendship in Oxygen.
>
> On October 6, we're hosting a night called Chapter 2. I need your help. I'm not only asking you to show up, but I'm asking you to be part of an unofficial leadership team on Wednesday nights. I know that if the people in this room are on my team, together we can dramatically change the tenor of our whole youth ministry. None of us want this to be just a holy huddle.
>
> Tonight I'm asking you, effective now, to help use your influence to change the tenor of our youth gatherings. Starting Wednesday, October 6, we're launching a few new changes, but more than those pragmatic things, I need the people in this room to take ownership of it. Some of you may not even consider yourselves committed Christians, but I think we'd all agree that authentic friendship is necessary in communicating the message of Christ. Together we can begin, not an American Revolution, but a friendship revolution here at Oxygen.

Right after my Paul Revere charge, I had a few student leaders share their own thoughts about boosting the friendliness factor in our group. I had selected the students ahead of time because they each carried weight in different social circles. If you want to create an epidemic of authentic friendliness, you have to involve several different influential students who will echo the worth and validity of your cause. Remember, what people are not up on, they're down on. It's important to win your students' hearts and then solidify your vision by enthusiastically enlisting them to take ownership.

As with all important meetings that you want to feel personal, I suggest you host this meeting away from the church—in your home, if possible. Serve light refreshments, and conclude the meeting by requesting that everyone fill out a response sheet before leaving. On the sheet, list any specific teams or projects you need help with, and ask the students to check off areas where they feel like they could get involved.

Remember, any major change in the culture or climate of a youth ministry needs to be strategically created through small group involvement before it ever goes to the entire group. That's where I think we've blown it so many times in youth ministry. The power of the pulpit is severely overrated. Students are "listened out." Lives are rarely changed by passively sitting through a youth night or message. But there is good news! Teenagers are *not* "involved out." If you can make them understand how important they are to the overall success of the changes in your group, you are on your way to having a whole new youth ministry in just a few months.

I know it might seem easier to implement a few changes and dive straight into a big Chapter 2 night, but if you don't take the time and effort to host those meetings, your results will be disappointing. In youth ministry, we often forget that it's not the event, it's the process leading up to the event that matters most.

Influencing Influencers

"I first met Jon when he was in junior high through a guy named Caleb in our youth group. Jon had recently moved to town and would come and play football with us periodically. At the end of Jon's sophomore year, Caleb invited me to speak at their school's FCA (Fellowship of Christian Athletes), and Jon committed his life to the Lord. He was an all-star football player and moved to town to be coached by a man who was a former college football coach. He began attending youth group, and we would go to the games and cheer him and the other guys on. Some of his fellow teammates called him 'baby Jesus.' But as a result of his commitment, approximately fifty students began attending our youth ministry. We've continued to love and support him, and today he plays for a college football team in South Carolina. I've learned that in youth ministry, we must 'influence the influencers, and they will make an influence.' "

—Darren Hileman, youth ministry veteran and college professor in Phoenixville, Pennsylvania

Step 4

Host a Chapter 2 night and simultaneously launch your S.I.P.

> If your group is struggling with cliquish behavior, you might also want to plan a "Death of Mr. Clique" night before your Chapter 2 night.
> See pages 67-79 for more on battling cliques.

It was our big night! We'd promoted it for three weeks and as the doors opened, I felt of mixture a fear and excitement. My goal that evening wasn't so much attendance as it was *feeling*. I wanted the atmosphere of the room to really feel different, more upbeat, friendly, energetic. We had greeters at the door, our students acted as row hosts, our new guest reception was ready to roll (Chapter 3 will tell you more about this), our hang-out area was complete with some simple entertainment, and our program for the night was carefully planned. But, as my years of youth ministry experience have taught me, *things don't always turn out the way you expect*. As I paused briefly before we began, there was no denying the knot in the pit of my stomach.

I took one more deep breath, lunged forward to head to the front, and almost ran over an excited middle school student who was running from the other direction. "Hey, Jeanne," he blurted out, "This is so cool. Counting the guys at the door, I've had eight people say hi to me!" He ran away, in his middle school state of euphoric confusion, off to look for number nine. No matter what else happened that evening, that encounter became my small gift from God and reassured me that we were really winning.

I've learned that it's not just the socially inept kids or middle school kids who unashamedly confess their need for a feeling of family and friendship; "cool" kids need to feel welcomed and loved too. Former pro athlete Bo Jackson, spoke out about his emptiness, admitting that no amount of athletic ability or fame could fill up the hole filled only by family. In his autobiography, *Bo Knows Bo*, Jackson wrote, "We never had enough food. But at

> *"All they really want is for someone to listen, to learn their names, and to make them feel loved."*

least I could beat on other kids and steal their lunch money...But I couldn't steal a father. I couldn't steal a father's hug when I needed one. I couldn't steal a father's...whipping when I needed one." That's exactly what Chapter 2 nights are all about: an attempt to transform the youth service into a place where both the young Bo Jacksons and the acne-plagued middle school students can come each week to feel the warmth of family and Christ's love. It's no secret: There are teenagers walking into your youth ministries who are victims of broken homes. They don't long for another video game or even to sleep with their high school's hottest guy or girl. All they really want is for someone to listen, to learn their names, and to make them feel loved.

Years ago I listened to an interview between my friend Josh McDowell and a representative of Playboy. Despite their obvious differences of opinion, they both managed to agree on one point—a point that I believe accurately portrays the need for relationships: "Today's culture is not so much experiencing a *sexual revolution* as it is *a revolution in the way they search for intimacy.*" Among all this discussion of logistics, please understand that the point of these seven steps is to make your youth ministry a viable option in a teen's search for intimacy.

The ingredients were simple. We implemented our new door greeters, guest cards, guest reception, and a few other pragmatic upgrades. We worked hard to make the worship music the best it could be with our sincere but mildly-talented musicians. Most importantly, the energy in the room was just what we had prayed for. Loud Christian music pumped as teenagers wandered in, and the student leaders (whom I'd asked to start showing up ten minutes early each week) did their thing. For the first time, the room really sounded alive. The jocks were talking to the computer geeks. The home-school girls were laughing with a group of cheerleaders. I sighed.

The Chapter 2 night included the following key elements:

• We showed video interviews with kids from a few of our local high schools. They were all asked one question: "If you ever went to a church gathering for teenagers, what would you be looking for?"

- Students presented a humorous, original skit called "How *not* to treat guests at Oxygen."

- I spoke for about five minutes on why we had called the night Chapter 2. I talked about how Christ prioritized friendships. I made it clear that we wanted the evening in Oxygen to launch a brand new era of friendship and acceptance—we wanted our youth ministry to be a place where they could feel comfortable inviting friends.

- We did a brief original drama depicting the importance of Christ-honoring friendship. We simply created a picture on stage of the day-to-day struggles teenagers deal with in their search for genuine friendship. We made sure the script had the two key ingredients—humor and sentiment.

- We closed the evening with student speakers. Before the meeting, I had selected five key students to speak from their hearts about the importance of this new era in Oxygen. They challenged the other students to make the night a true beginning, a valid Chapter 2. Each student only spoke for two to three minutes, but it was powerful. One of the students was a prominent athlete whom I'd asked to share about his own pain from a divorce that had happened recently in his family. I challenged him to tell the group that it hurts and to emphasize how much he needed Oxygen to feel like a family. Another girl shared about her struggle with anorexia. Though she appeared to have the world by the tail, she let the group know that she needed people at Oxygen to help her feel like she was accepted and to assist her toward better health. A shy, quiet guy spoke out about how he was always scared to say anything, but how badly he wanted someone to be his friend. He admitted that he even laid his clothes out for Oxygen the night before because it was that important to him. The final

---

Snacks—a Secret to Success

"We basically strive to connect with the students who visit our youth ministry from the time they walk into our facility until the moment they leave. We offer a full-color visitor brochure that includes a coupon to our Snack Shop. Adding a snack shop was a great addition that allows for students to 'hang out' and get to know one another. Our visitor retention rate has drastically increased since we began to focus more on our guests' needs and less on our wants!"

—Todd Bishop, youth pastor in Valley Stream, New York

person shared that although he had been raised in the church, he was still waiting for the whole "God thing to come alive" in his own life. He said he'd stopped attending Oxygen because he felt so much like he was "on the outside looking in." As each teenager shared, you could have heard a pin drop.

• I closed that night by telling one of my favorite stories. Jesus was a parable teller, and during my years in youth ministry I've followed his example. I don't know if the story that follows really happened, but regardless, the point is meaningful. A Chinese student who attended college in America was befriended by a Christian girl, and in time the Chinese student became a Christian herself. When her pastor asked the Chinese student what prompted her to give her heart to Christ, the pastor might have expected to hear a profound answer…but it didn't come. The girl wasn't won over by deep theological truths shown to her by campus intellectuals. She didn't come to believe in Christ because of a compelling, eloquent sermon. Her powerful answer epitomizes true youth ministry. She simply explained, "My Christian friend has used this year to build a bridge from her heart to mine. And today I let Jesus walk over it."

Did you catch the impact of that last line? It's a good job description of 21st century youth ministry. We just build friendship bridges from our heart to theirs—hoping that one day, they will let Jesus walk over it. So as I close out this segment, maybe it would be a great place for you to stop reading for a minute and talk with the Lord. After all, none of us wants to stand before the Lord one day with an enlarged ministry, but a shrunken heart. In your journey of building a welcoming youth ministry, how good are you at building "heart bridges" that Jesus can walk over?

Step 5

Avoid the rental car syndrome.

Have you ever driven a rental car? As I travel around the nation communicating in different venues, I occasionally use rental cars. While some of them have been nice, I have never once taken a rental car for

> *"Do whatever it takes to make your Chapter 2 team feel sincerely appreciated and motivated for the long haul. Without this vital link, your friendship culture will soon become about as powerful as a rusted-out rental car."*

a wash, oil-change, or mechanical checkup. Why? The answer is obvious—I don't care enough about the car to bother taking care of it. *I have no sense of ownership.*

I think the implications of building a friendship culture are obvious. Your students need desperately to *own* this whole concept of making your youth group meetings more visitor-friendly. If not, the air will very soon come out of your tires. This whole area of ownership is difficult in youth ministry because many kids today have a problem with commitment and follow-through. So don't get discouraged when people let you down, fail to follow through, and bail out. Welcome to the real world of youth ministry! In spite of this reality, it is still absolutely imperative that you work with students to make sure they *own* simple parts of your new friendship focus, much like they did on your Chapter 2 night. Aspects of ownership can range from door greeters, row hosts, video creation, skits, testimonies, follow-up letters, and phone calls. Just sensitively try to match people with areas they would be good at and enjoy. And if you want to keep ownership a signature of your new focus, be sure to remember that whatever conduct gets rewarded, gets repeated. That means be quick to catch what they're doing right, and praise, praise, praise!

Because continued ownership will create the need for some form of occasional refueling and realigning, consider hosting Chapter 2 leadership meetings once every couple of months. Choose a time that is most convenient for your participants, and do your homework to make sure these meetings feel like a true "Appreciation Pep Rally." I know, I know—people should do these things for the Lord, not for the appreciation of other people. And that is absolutely right, but let me tell you a very important secret: While you are trying to create a culture of "family" among your youth ministry, you also need to prioritize creating a feeling of "family" among your key leaders. Do whatever it takes to make your Chapter 2 team feel sincerely appreciated and motivated for the long haul. Without this vital link, your friendship culture will soon become about as powerful as a rusted-out rental car.

Step 6

When you get bored, tired, or discouraged...keep going.

When I was younger, my dad used to tell me, "Jeanne, no plan will work unless you do." He was 100 percent right. When it comes to creating a visitor-friendly youth ministry, you must remember, "Don't wait for your boat to come in. Swim out to it!" The truth is that nothing is going to change in the friendship fabric of your youth ministry unless you choose to pay the costly, disciplined price to make it happen. Please trust me, it will be more than worth every sacrifice and will cost you more effort on the front end as you get things started than it will in the months to follow.

Regardless of whether you are a volunteer youth leader or a paid youth pastor, we all know that youth ministry at its best can sometimes get pretty boring, weary, and discouraging. That's why I wanted to include these simple words of encouragement to motivate you for the long haul. Youth ministry is full of good starters but very few good finishers. I challenge you to be not only one of those people who start efforts to make student ministry more visitor-friendly and welcoming, but one of those rare souls who actually *keep going.* I often tell teenagers that "right choices eventually bring right emotions." Just like you, I often have to remind myself to keep going, even when I don't feel like it.

Fifth Quarters

"Every Friday night, after the local football game concludes, we host a Fifth Quarter party. The game usually concludes around 9 p.m., and kids have about two hours before their curfew is up. We just have music, food, and random prizes. It's great for teenagers to invite friends in who wouldn't normally come to church, and it gives our sponsors (adult volunteers) a chance to build relationships outside of Wednesday night."

—Tom Buchanan, youth pastor in Robinson, Illinois

When I become bored with calling kids and tired of picking up all the pieces, I remind myself that my right choices will eventually bring back my right emotions. When I get discouraged at the number of people who flake out on their responsibilities and quit, I remind myself again that no matter how gratifying the idea of throwing in the towel might feel to me right then, I can't afford to give in to those feelings. And I keep going. When I become so discouraged that I can hardly pull myself through one more youth service, feeling like all I get for my hard work is criticism and misunderstanding, I show up for the meeting with a smile on my face anyway. Yes, as tough as it sometimes is, I have come to realize that my Christ-honoring right choices will eventually bring right emotions. I would have quit youth ministry a thousand frustrations ago if I had allowed my emotions of boredom, weariness, or discouragement to win. The acronym H.A.L.T. has been helpful to me as I've evaluated myself during down times; it reminds me not to make any major decision or reverses when I am **H**ungry, **A**ngry, **L**onely, or **T**ired. When you are tempted to back off in your efforts to create a Christ-honoring friendship culture among your youth ministry and the teenagers you care about, just throw up a prayer to the Lord and ask him to help you check your levels and readjust your focus. Remember—H.A.L.T.!

Host an Andrew Night every six weeks.

Do you remember Andrew in the New Testament? He was one of Jesus' twelve disciples and one of my personal favorites. The reason why I'd nominate Andrew for the "Disciple of the Year" award is not why you might think. I mean, it's obvious that Peter was a much better upfront guy, John was better relationally, and Judas had them all beat on keeping the books. So what was Andrew's most notable achievement? *He brought Peter to meet the Lord.* Andrew was a bringer. He probably didn't even try to match verbal wits with Peter. He just knew that if he could bring him to Jesus, things would probably work out.

I remind the kids about Andrew every once in a while. I tell them they don't have to possess all the evangelistic talent of a Billy Graham to be an

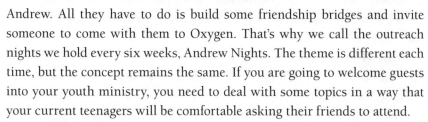

Seven Steps to Change Everything
1. Pull together a diverse group of key students and say, "Talk to me."
2. Create an S.I.P. with target Velcro points.
3. Host a Paul Revere meeting for key influencers.
4. Host a Chapter 2 night, and simultaneously launch your S.I.P.
5. Avoid the rental car syndrome.
6. When you get bored, tired, or discouraged...keep going.
7. Host an Andrew Night every six weeks.

Andrew. All they have to do is build some friendship bridges and invite someone to come with them to Oxygen. That's why we call the outreach nights we hold every six weeks, Andrew Nights. The theme is different each time, but the concept remains the same. If you are going to welcome guests into your youth ministry, you need to deal with some topics in a way that your current teenagers will be comfortable asking their friends to attend.

These Andrew Nights do not need to take a million hours of work. Just try to do the following:

- Build the night around a theme that is an easy connector for non-churched kids. This would not be the night to deal with the religious symbolism of the third toe in Daniel's vision. Pick themes like relationships, failure, or fears.

- Make use of creative communication techniques like skits, drama, video, or student sharing.

- Use language that will connect with visitors, like, "Around Oxygen, we don't care what religion you are a part of; we're not into religion. We just focus on relationships" or "It doesn't matter what your church background is; we're just really glad to have you with us tonight."

- Provide simple, inexpensive promotional materials for your students to use when inviting friends. If you can, get students with graphic art skills to design your promotional materials.

- Do simple follow-up on your guests after each Andrew Night (see Chapter 4 for ideas.) When it comes down to it, we shouldn't ask Jesus to keep sending us guests if we don't take care of them after they arrive.

I guarantee that once your kids see that you are putting thought and prayer into making Andrew Nights "cool," they will begin asking their friends to come. The sobering reality is that most of them don't ask friends to attend youth service because they are secretly afraid that the night will be boring, embarrassing, or irrelevant.

Myth-Busting

Reflecting back on my first wake-up call with Ben, I think that the youth ministry leadership culture is filled with unspoken perceptions that really damage our effectiveness. Without bursting your bubble, allow me to dispel a few of the myths I've heard repeatedly from youth leaders through the years:

Myth #1—Teenagers don't come back to our youth services because of me. After all, if I was really praying enough, the results will be automatic.

As I travel the country speaking in leadership forums, I have met countless amazing youth leaders with a deep authentic love for Jesus Christ. As I talk with them, I hear their words reflecting a deep commitment to both Christ and to their students. Yet time after time, these same leaders tell me about their sense of failure in the youth ministry arena. They talk openly about their inability to motivate their students to bring friends to the weekly youth gathering. Although their wording varies, each sincere leader seems to think his or her challenges in youth ministry come from "not being called" or "not having enough scriptural knowledge." I understand because I was once in that boat. Back then I tried to create a thriving youth ministry by praying a little harder and buying a few too many tickets to spiritual guilt trips. I could have been the poster child for Spiritually Sincere Youth Leaders Who Are Still Clueless! I loved the Lord with all my heart, but rather than having the ability to grow a youth ministry, I seemed to have a talent for making it plateau. (I'm sure *you* don't have that spiritual gift.) The agonizing truth is that it is possible to be deeply spiritual and *still struggle* to create a thriving and welcoming youth ministry.

Myth #2—Teenagers don't come back to a youth ministry due to the lack of a good communicator up front and a quality program.

Remember that Group survey I mentioned earlier? You know—the one where kids placed "a welcoming atmosphere where I can be myself" at the top end and an "entertaining ministry approach" at the bottom? You *should* try to make your program top notch, but don't fool yourself into thinking that a cool program is the key.

A little planning and a little effort really do go a long way. I've given you seven simple steps that you can begin implementing as jump-starters for your group. Don't overwhelm yourself by trying to implement all of them at once. You might want to take some time and share a few of the steps with your leaders or sponsors, and allow them to get creative and excited and even take ownership of a few ideas. Whatever you do, remember: None of it will work unless you do. It's a lot like moving a large object. At first, it takes more effort and force, but once you get the ball rolling, it begins to take care of itself. These secrets will help you not only grow the size of your group, but give your teenagers a place where they always feel welcomed.

Java and Tunes

"In the basement of our church, we built a coffee shop for kids to start hanging out. Locally, lots of teenagers put together 'garage bands,' and *they* wanted to start playing. So once a month we started having coffee house/concert night. It's brought in a lot of kids, and recently one of them came to our youth service, and we were discussing Christ's love. She started to cry and said, 'I like coming here because it feels real.' It made me realize that at the end of the night, it doesn't matter if the monitors don't work or if one of the songs was off key. Students were impacted."

—Rachelle Sumrall, youth ministry worship leader in South Bend, Indiana

Now What? Ideas

Use these ideas to put the principles in this chapter into action:

- Read Acts 1:1—9:31, looking for ways the early church epitomized some of the principles in this chapter. How did growth occur in their community? How can your group rely on the Holy Spirit to take strategic steps to developing a thriving culture?

- Contact city hall to get some demographic information. Find out approximately how many teenagers live in your city, then write the number on a map of your city. Post the map in your office as a prayer reminder to you while you take steps to reach out to more teenagers.

- Make a list of students you'd like to invite to your first Talk to Me meeting.

- Set a date and begin putting your plans in motion.

- Reflect on your own weekly youth gathering—ask yourself what changes you could make to create a few true Velcro points.

- Take the time to create your own S.I.P. for enhancing friendliness in your youth gathering.

- Begin to plan your own Paul Revere meeting.

- Host your own Chapter 2 night.

- Provide students with some simple, inexpensive promotional materials to pass out prior to your first Andrew Night.

- Learn about other creative strategies for growing your ministry by reading these church leadership resources from Group Publishing, Inc.: An Unstoppable Force by Erwin McManus, The Externally Focused Church by Rick Rusaw and Eric Swanson, Igniting Passion in Your Church by Steve Ayers.

_____

_____

_____

{ We have freshly baked
chocolate chip cookies,
and they're just for you. }

Hosting Your Own Guest Reception

Imagine this scenario—a teenage guy looks pretty normal from all superficial appearances, but in reality he's experiencing slow, internal bleeding that will eventually take his life if the condition isn't addressed. His whole family, sensing that something is terribly wrong, begs the young man to visit a medical facility to get some help. But he repeatedly refuses, telling everyone around him, "I feel OK and besides, I don't like doctors and hospitals."

Months pass, and to the relief of his whole family, he agrees one evening to visit the emergency room of the local hospital. When he walks in, no one acknowledges him. He walks to the counter to make his presence known, but the staff seem preoccupied with each other. He clears his throat, shuffling nervously to gain their attention. Finally, one of the medical personnel gives him a token greeting, right before walking into another room laughing with one of the doctors. Minutes later, a female medical technician makes eye contact with our ailing friend. Awkwardly, he attempts to introduce himself to her, as a way of asking for help. The attendant responds coolly and tells him to have a seat in the small, crowded hospital waiting area. He sits down hesitantly. It seems that everyone else there somehow knows each other personally, but no one speaks to him.

Over an hour passes. None of the medical staff makes any effort to personally connect or respond to the young man. They just seem to think his medical problems will get better by his sheer presence inside the hospital. Because he has nothing else to do, he observes the medical procedures that are going on all around him. He doesn't understand everything he sees. The medical language is foreign, and the procedures are too complex for him to make sense of them. He isn't sure whether he feels the people in the hospital are unfriendly, weird, or just confusing. Amidst all these emotions, one of the doctors passes a container around the hospital waiting area, asking all the guests to contribute to the ongoing expenses of the hospital.

Finally, after over an hour of medical talk and procedures that our friend does not understand, one of the medical assistants behind the desk looks up and thanks him for coming. Confused, our ill teenager stands to leave. No one has connected with him personally or acted like they wanted to know what brought him to the hospital in the first place. Nor has anyone tried to assist him in any concrete way. They seemed quite content that he merely visited the hospital.

As he starts to leave the hospital that evening, he is more confused and turned off than ever. He wasn't so sure he wanted to come in the first place. He didn't know anybody there and honestly didn't think he needed any medical attention. Now, after his initial visit to the hospital, he is even more convinced that the hospital is both irrelevant and impersonal. Just as the door shuts behind him, the doctor, in a detached voice, calls out, "Be sure to come back next week!"

"Fat chance," the young man says to himself sarcastically. "I never should have let myself get conned into coming in the first place." And as he drives

---

From Visitors to Guests

"What are the feelings of the hometown crowd toward the visiting team? We typically don't like them. We don't even put their name on the scoreboard and can't wait until they get on the bus and head out of town. Visitors are not welcome. What do many churches call people who have never been to their church or youth group? You got it: *visitors!* I prefer to call them *guests*. A guest in my home gets the nicest room, the fluffiest pillow, and the best towels. A guest is worthy of the best treatment and special attention. It's a minor adjustment that sends a big message to those who are there for the first time. "

—Dean Hawk, youth worker and youth ministry speaker in Colorado Springs, Colorado

> *"We excitedly cultivate relationships with each other, hoping somehow that guests will push their way into our cliquish friendship circles."*

away, the entire medical staff inside the hospital celebrates about the number of visitors they had that night. They quickly e-mail their visitors record to other hospitals around them, and a well-respected medical magazine finds out and asks them to write an article on how they've built their attendance.

Amidst their excitement, there is a grave problem. Unbeknown to them, their ill guest has left the medical facility with a greater determination to "never be caught dead in a hospital again." His expression is haunting, for though he does not realize it, he continues to die from his untreated internal problem. Ironically, the next time he visits the hospital, he will arrive as a corpse. It's tragic that the medical personnel didn't pay more attention to making sure his visit to their facility really did count.

Tragic as this simple analogy is, it is painfully accurate when we parallel it to how many youth ministries respond to their guests. We work so hard to get people inside our doors, but we put very little effort into strategically connecting with them and making their first visit with us a positive one. We speak church language and are pretty clueless when it comes to formulating a plan on how to make guests feel valued. We excitedly cultivate relationships with each other, hoping somehow that guests will push their way into our cliquish friendship circles. Then to our astonishment, our percentage of guests who return the next week is low.

With this problem in mind, I pulled a group of students together years ago and asked them what we could do to make it more comfortable for them to bring guests. Lots of great suggestions were given, but perhaps one of the most important ideas that came from this brainstorming session was hosting a simple weekly guest reception. For over twenty-five years now, I have hosted weekly visitor receptions for our guests. Though our presentation style has changed through the years, the overall format has remained much the same. A guest reception is simple to host as part of your regular youth meeting, and you may discover it will be your most valuable eight to ten minutes of the night.

Why Take Time Out for Guests?

Through the years, we've always taken time out to make our guests feel welcome. We usually set aside time for guests during the announcements and offering segment of our youth meeting. We use this time for two reasons. First, we want to host it near the start of the meeting so our guests feel authentically welcomed early on in the evening. Second, we prefer that our first-timers not feel turned off by requests for their money during the offering.

Let me briefly share with you how we've done our weekly guest receptions. After two or three up-tempo worship songs, the music leader says something like, "We're really excited to have all of you with us tonight. We're especially glad to have our first time guests. If this happens to be your first night with us at Oxygen, please just sit down in the chair right behind you! We'd like to come around and introduce ourselves. In a few minutes, we'd like to give you a small information sheet that we'll exchange for some free food and a video presentation." First-time guests stay seated while the other students make their way through the group, looking for seated guests to introduce themselves to. We play music in the background to help create an exciting atmosphere of fun and energy. The week prior to beginning this important practice, I had briefly explained to our regular attendees the "what and why" behind our new guest reception.

As the students mill around creating a warm, party atmosphere, a few teenagers pass out guest clipboards to the visitors. Each small clipboard has a guest reception card and a pen attached to it (see page 51 for more on creating your own guest reception card). At the conclusion of the two to three minute "greet our guests" time, the music calms down, and everyone is asked to return to their seats. From the front, the guests are welcomed warmly again and instructed to fill out the guest card. The emcee then explains, "In a minute, you'll be able to exchange your card for free food and get a chance to hear what we're all about around here."

While the visitors complete their guest cards, we always make a priority announcement. This is the one key announcement that we want stressed for the evening. Then the emcee may say something like, "OK, we're going to ask that everyone please stand back up now. We're about to begin one of the highlights of Oxygen each week: our guest reception. If you're with us tonight for the first time, just grab your clipboard and follow John out the side door (point in the direction). We have free food for you, and we want to show you a short video. We want you to know that we're so much more than just a Wednesday night meeting. If you came as someone's guest tonight, feel free to take that person with you—but if you came alone, we

> ### Circular Welcome: Pizza, Frisbees, Cookies!
> "We give our visitors a free personal pan pizza and throw them a free Frisbee during the youth service while applauding their attendance. We always follow up with a special delivery of homemade cookies, thanking them for coming."
> —Drew Massey, youth pastor in Hannibal, Missouri

promise you won't feel out of place. You'll only be gone about five minutes, and then you'll rejoin all of us. As the worship team starts to play, all of our amazing guests as well as those who brought them, please exit out this door and head to our guest reception."

Making Everyone Feel at Home

Sound like a lot of detail? I know it really is, but through the years, I've learned that a few small statements can make it or break it when it comes to making visitors feel comfortable. Here are a few key things to remember as you attempt to help your visitors feel comfortable:

- Make sure everyone in the room is standing as you ask your guests to exit.

- Be sure to mention the new guest reception to your core students the week before you launch it so they know to go with their guests.

- Keep the music upbeat, whether live or on CD, so the energy stays high.

- Set up the guest reception area so it is relatively easy to access from where you normally meet.

There are lots of different ways to put on your guest reception. Just make sure you focus on this important principle: *Your guests need to feel like you genuinely care about them.* Just saying hi and beaming a friendly smile isn't enough. They need you to go the extra mile to show them how excited you are that they showed up. You may choose to host a reception once a month or even to make it a special couple of minutes right when they're sitting down at the start of your meeting. Just keep in mind that the goal is to create a tenor of warmth, excitement, and friendliness for all guests. However you decide to do it, the important thing is that you focus on aesthetics that will put any visitor at ease.

Where Two or More Are Gathered, There Should Be Food!

When visitors enter our guest reception room, they're welcomed by greeters and immediately directed to the refreshment table. Through the years of hosting guest receptions, we have served a wide variety of food. When our budget was tight, I recruited a couple of grandmothers in the church to make us chocolate chip cookies each week. I made sure these women legitimately saw this as a ministry and offered to give them a monthly allowance to cover their costs. Those cookies became the raving hit of our whole youth group! The teenagers always enjoyed hearing me say, "If you're a guest tonight, we have some of the greatest, warm, freshly baked chocolate chip cookies that you've ever tasted right behind those doors, and they're just for you!" (Of course, we regularly had to stop other kids from sneaking into the reception to steal the cookies!)

When the budget was not so tight, we served pizza and pop. Sometimes a local pizza place would provide the pizza for free as long as we made sure their logo was visible each week at the youth gathering. We usually pre-cut the pizza and pre-poured the pop so visitors could quickly grab it as they walked in the door.

After grabbing their snacks, the visitors take a seat, and the host of the guest reception officially welcomes them again and tells them how great it is to have them visit the youth group. The host should be one of your sharpest student leaders because this person is crucial in creating a good first impression. Before launching into the meeting, the host asks everyone to pass in their guest registration card with the completed information. Getting these cards is crucial so that you can execute the visitor follow-up as discussed in Chapter 4.

Take a Moment to Eliminate the Unknown

We always show a short five-minute video in the guest reception to explain who we are and to give some background information about our beliefs. If you don't have the resources to create a video, you could use slides, a PowerPoint presentation, or just have a student speak to the group. The important thing to keep in mind is that most churches have traditions, ceremonies, and behaviors that come across as pretty foreign (and sometimes even *weird*) to the average non-Christian teenager. For example, imagine someone who has not grown up in church hearing the words, "washed in the blood of the lamb." What would they think?! Other practices like raising hands during worship, reciting a liturgical prayer, singing memorized songs, or even taking communion can seem foreign and bizarre to a first-time visitor. This presentation time gives you a moment to bridge the gap between those who are "in the know" and those who just walked into a totally new environment.

In your video, slideshow, or spoken presentation, follow these guidelines:

• Say something like, "Here at [the name of your youth ministry], we're not into religion. We're into relationships. We don't care what your denominational background is, what church you attend on Sunday mornings, or if you don't attend church at all. We're just glad you showed up tonight, and we want to help you know Jesus in a more exciting and real way." This type of statement is key in making sure guests feel welcome and nondefensive. I can't tell you how many times one of the teenagers in the group would whisper to me before the service, "Don't forget the denomination line tonight. I've brought a friend with me who needs to hear it!"

• Highlight key aspects of the youth group meeting that they are about to experience (such as worship music, drama, or games).

• Stress both verbally and with pictures the relational and friendship aspect of your ministry. Paint a clear picture that you are not just a youth group—you're a youth *family*.

• Because our strategy of discipleship pivots around small groups, we briefly highlight them in our video. Whatever your format for discipleship is, reference it and, if possible, hand out something in print that goes into more detail.

> *"Have enough character to work just as hard for a small crowd as you would for a large one."*

- Explain any aspects of the youth group meeting that might confuse non-churched students, such as recited prayers, singing worship songs, lifting hands, taking communion, or anything else that may seem normal to your church but could feel threatening to kids who've never been to your group before.

- One of the most common misconceptions of Christianity that guests have is that it is boring. So, show video footage or pictures of retreats, activities, or special events in order to show students how much fun your group has.

- Include quick, five-second testimonials from a few guys and girls about different aspects of your youth ministry like "I enjoy coming because the teaching from the Bible relates to my life," "People are so friendly here," or "You don't have to look or act a certain way to have people accept you."

- Conclude the video or presentation with slower music and a statement like, "So from all of us at [your youth ministry], let us tell you again how honored we are to have you with us tonight. We hope you show up more often, so we can get to know you better. As you go back into the meeting, remember that Jesus said he came to earth to give all of us life and life more abundantly. We hope you experience that kind of exciting, abundant life while you're here tonight."

Though this may seem like a lot of content, a good script and a bit of editing can easily make your video five minutes or less.

Wrap-Up Smoothly

The reception host should wrap things up by saying, "It's time to return to the service. As you exit, we have some materials about our small groups for you to take with you. We'd love for you to visit soon. There are lots of exciting activities coming up and lots of great people to get to know around here. Again, thanks so much for coming!" All the guests should then make their way back into the main meeting area. When they enter, we usually have the emcee say something like, "Hey, our visitors are coming back from the guest reception. Let's all stand and clap for them as they return, and let them know how glad we are to have them with us tonight."

Please don't let the details about the guest reception overwhelm you. With some simple planning and delegation, this will not be highly demanding or difficult to pull off. Like many things in life, it takes a little bit of extra effort in the beginning, but it will reap great dividends in the future. The guest reception should be about eight minutes long, and eventually it will become so natural that you'll wonder what you did without it.

An Invaluable Eight Minutes

I still remember when we hosted our very first guest reception. I had made an arrangement with a few of my student leaders, saying, "We don't want our guests to feel stupid or singled out. So until we start having enough guests to make this OK, would you attend the reception each week? We need warm bodies in the room, and they don't need to know if you're a guest or not." That first evening, we had two whole visitors! We rolled out the red carpet for them as though there were hundreds. Perhaps that is one of youth ministry's greatest secrets of success: Have enough character to work just as hard for a small crowd as you would for a large one.

Something surprising began to happen the next week. I don't think we ever had just two visitors again after that first night. Our visitor numbers began to slowly climb. Visitors brought their friends back the next week and proudly ushered them into the guest reception that they had just attended the week before. And beyond that, my core students in the youth ministry began to ask more friends to attend. Why? They became less inhibited to invite friends when they realized we were hosting something each week that made their guests feel taken care

> ### Don't Single Me Out!
> "Even though I am a licensed minister, I enter almost every service with the mind of a new person. I visited a church once on a morning where, in all honesty, I was glad to be a visitor! I didn't have to get on stage, I talked to people only when I wanted to, and I could leave right after the service! Two minutes into the service, the pastor asked me to stand up and introduce myself. I decided I didn't ever want to be a visitor again!"
> —Bobbi Lanham, associate pastor in Mendon, Massachusetts

of. In the words of one of our students, "Even if my friends don't like the message, it's pretty tough not to like all the personal attention we give them around here."

When was the last time you were a visitor? Have you stepped into another church, attended a civic event, or gone to a party where you didn't know many people? Think for a minute about what it feels like—awkward, scary, tense. Now think of all the teenagers outside your church walls. There are millions in the world who are outside the church doors, but for you and me, my friend, it is the one or two who wander in and need someone to hear them—someone to not forget what it was like to be outside of the door.

> **Your guests need to feel like you genuinely care about them.**

Now What? Ideas

Use these ideas to put the principles in this chapter into action:

- Visit a church you've never been to. Step inside the shoes of a non-Christian or spiritual seeker. What is the experience like? Did you feel welcomed? What could have made the experience better for you?

- Brainstorm with your team of student leaders about how to create your own guest reception. Work to draw up a guest reception S.I.P.

  ☐ Who will host it?

  ☐ Where will you host it?

  ☐ What food will you serve and how will you get it?

  ☐ Brainstorm together on what should be included in the content of the presentation.

  ☐ Assign two people to write the final script of the five-minute reception presentation (on video or live).

  ☐ Set a target date when you will do a test run of the reception.

  ☐ Set a date for when you plan to host your first guest reception.

- Create a guest registration card.

  ☐ Make print large enough to see clearly.

  ☐ Use either a postcard size or half sheet.

  ☐ Print on heavy card stock paper (makes it easier to write on)—then make copies as needed.

  ☐ Information needed on card:

   1. A cool logo or design at the top or in a corner.

   2. Name, address, phone number, e-mail, school, grade, birthday, and who brought or invited them.

  ☐ Before you print it—have a few of your teenagers look at it and tell you if it's easy to understand and if it looks appealing.

Now What? Idea

continued

• Consider making free Bibles available to guests who may not have a Bible of their own, such as *The Youth Bible* available from Group Publishing, Inc.

_____

_____

_____

_____

_____

_____

_____

_____

_____

{We're glad to have you with us.}

Operation Follow-Up

I've experienced a lot of high points during my thirty-five years in youth ministry. One of the most exciting highs was a citywide youth campaign we sponsored in Illinois called Revolution. It was the brainchild of Dan Valentine, one of our amazing youth leaders. We had billboards all over the city and passed out thousands of invitations in local high schools where Dan hosted all-school assemblies. Our team worked on this exciting youth outreach event for over one year.

The results were staggering. In three nights of youth services in our church's main sanctuary, we had a total of over twelve thousand teenagers attend! We imported no outside music or talent; it was led by just the "home team." Each night, hundreds of sincere teenagers decided to begin a relationship with Christ. I must admit I had never been a part of a youth event so citywide and powerful in its impact, yet the most amazing part to me was that Revolution was totally promoted and produced by *us*—our church's local youth ministry team. I remember the last night thinking we would not be able to hold the number of students who would undoubtedly show up the following Wednesday night for our youth service. It was a great problem to anticipate.

*" With consistent follow-up, a local youth ministry **can** experience a strong retention rate of new believers and visitors. "*

We passed out colorful flyers at the closing Friday night service of Revolution as everyone left that evening, inviting them to a drama we were planning the next Wednesday night. We used the drama's title and message to target new Christians. In an effort to make sure that none of the other youth leaders in the city felt like we were trying to steal their kids, we didn't mail out any personal letters or invitations to students. We laid low on personal phone calls too because we didn't want to do anything that would appear as dividing the body of Christ or taking unfair advantage of our position after the success of Revolution. But amidst these concerns, I can promise you that we did our homework on preparing for the following week's youth night. Besides that, the promotional pieces we passed out at the door of Revolution's last night were sharp and appealing.

You can only imagine our enthusiasm as we worked toward the next Wednesday night meeting. We excitedly wondered if we would have the space to accommodate all the new believers who would be attending. Late Tuesday night, I remember lingering in the sanctuary after the final drama practice had concluded. I walked among the rows of seats, sincerely praying for the continuation of last week's miraculous success. I envisioned the room being packed with teenagers in a way we had never seen before.

But when Wednesday night came, I tasted disappointment like I had not experienced in a long time. Most of our leadership team came early to pray that night, asking Jesus to continue the miraculous things we had witnessed the previous week. We welcomed the privilege of helping so many young teenage believers get a great start in their walk with Christ. I remember in my pep talk after we prayed together that I encouraged everyone to be ready to give up their seats if necessary.

The Christian music was pumping, and the greeters were told they could open the doors. We all glanced at the entrances, primed to introduce ourselves to the new Christians that would come flooding in—but then it happened. The doors opened, but no rushing herd of students poured in.

Our regular attendees showed up, looking around aimlessly for the masses of visitors they expected. Finally, we picked our stomachs up off the floor, realizing that the masses were apparently not showing up that night.

At the end of the night, we sat down with our spiritual tails between our legs. What was the final outcome that evening? Well, our youth service attendance that night was only slightly higher than the week before we had hosted Revolution. To make everything even more agonizing, we discovered in our guest reception that only a small number of our guests that night had even attended Revolution. About half of them had come as normal first time guests with another person in our youth ministry.

Now don't get me wrong: I know that just because students didn't show up at our youth service that next week doesn't mean they didn't make a genuine spiritual growth commitment. Yet new Christians *do* need a youth group that they can plug into so they can grow with other Christian teenagers. I had a hard time believing that most of those new Christians were already involved in another church in the city.

I'm often reminded that he who would make bread for others must first himself go through the mill. My disappointment after the spiritual high of Revolution sent me through the mill for several days. Hopefully, my experience will allow me to make some decent youth ministry "bread" for you right now. I relearned for the ninety-ninth time that aggressive outreach without equally aggressive follow-up will often produce disappointing results.

Following Revolution, I felt like a failure. I remember thinking, "Dan did a brilliant job on his end, but the Lord must have thought we weren't trustworthy enough to handle the results." It was during this season of personal head-bashing that I heard something about the world-changing Billy Graham Evangelistic Association that gave me a small degree of comfort amidst my huge sense of disappointment. While Billy Graham's crusade results are undeniably significant, only a very small percentage of those who commit their lives to Christ at Graham's events are integrated into a local church one year later. Even Billy Graham's team struggles to get the results they want! This helped remind me that sometimes our best efforts for Christ don't measure up to our prayers and dreams.

The Good News
After the Wake-Up Call

The good news is that with consistent follow-up, a local youth ministry *can* experience a strong retention rate of new believers and visitors. Rapid and age-appropriate follow-up from our local youth group is what we chose *not* to prioritize after Revolution to avoid causing any problems with some of the city's other youth groups. And as a result, we learned quickly that no matter how sincere a person's decision to follow Christ is, personal follow-up is absolutely necessary for a long-term spiritual harvest.

Allow me to share with you some of our simple strategies for follow-up; these strategies can be tailored to do follow-up with guests, fringe kids, and new Christians. Growing a friendly and welcoming youth ministry is not rocket science. It just requires your determination to implement some practices of personal contact with students and consistent follow-up.

Remember to start where you are. Don't focus on what you aren't doing or what you don't have. Rather, focus on your opportunity to initiate some new strategies that will make a world of difference. In *Teaching a Stone to Talk*, Annie Dillard wrote about the Crab Nebula in the Taurus constellation, saying, "It is a star in the process of exploding...It expands at the rate of seventy million miles a day." Yet, as Dillard noted, if you look at the Crab Nebula through a telescope, you see no movement at all. It doesn't seem to be budging, let alone exploding. A picture taken of the Crab Nebula ten years ago looks like a photo taken last night.

The Crab Nebula reminds me that even when it doesn't feel like it, my small efforts in youth ministry do create huge repercussions in God's invisible spiritual world. As you begin to implement some of the follow-up suggestions you are about to read, changes won't always be immediately apparent to your human eye. Remember that progress may not be obvious yet, but it is still happening—perhaps even at the rate of seventy million spiritual miles a day!

Having said that, let me jump into some valuable suggestions that really work. Just choose one or two to start at a time, and use them to enhance your new initiative to become the friendliest youth group in your city.

Sending Personal Letters, With or Without a Secretary

The starting place for Operation Follow-Up may be as simple as determining to send out personal welcome letters to your visitors each week. Teenagers today are so starved for family love and personal attention that even small gestures done consistently will make a *big* difference.

Start out by making sure your youth group has stationery that looks appealing to teenagers. Invite some teenagers or an adult in your church to design a simple letterhead, and then have a small group of teenagers look at it and give feedback. You'll get a look you really like free of charge! To cover printing costs, have copies made at an office supply/printing store, or determine what it would cost to have stationery printed professionally, and ask some adults in your church if they'd be willing to cover the cost. Make sure they understand the *why* behind the *what*. In other words, explain to them that you're trying to create a more welcoming atmosphere in your youth ministry that will be highly attractive to guests. Stress the bottom line of being able to impact more teenagers for Christ. I think you'll be pleasantly surprised how quickly adults in the church will cover expenses like this for youth!

The next step is getting the actual letter in the mail. I know you may be among the majority of people in youth ministry who do not have a full- or part-time secretary. Don't despair! There is an easy, effective way around this challenge. After creating stationery and a letter, begin to look for a reliable, detailed-oriented teenage or adult volunteer who could take care of this for you every week. This person needs to have average typing skills and be intelligent enough to be trained on creating a basic data-entry list or spreadsheet. Provide your volunteer with stationery, stamps, and a master copy of the letter. Also set up a time when he or she can regularly pick up the guest information cards after each youth meeting. Years before

It's in the Mail

"We always write letters to follow up on our visitors. We've learned, especially with middle schoolers, they don't like to be singled out in front of people, but they do like the attention of follow-up."

—Kellen Cochran, junior high youth pastor in Birmingham, Alabama

I ever had a secretary, I followed this process with great success. The volunteer I chose was very disciplined and conscientious. She'd photocopy the guest reception cards each week and regularly send out the letters within twenty-four hours of the guests' visit to our group.

Here are a few tips we've learned as we've refined the follow-up letter process:

- Always use stamps rather than a postage meter. Stamps visually communicate that it's a personal message.
- Keep the letter to one page in length.
- Thank them again for coming, and invite them to come back.
- Knowing that many parents will probably read the letter, make sure to communicate that the student is welcome to attend without changing his or her Sunday church or denominational preference.
- Include a personal P.S. at the bottom of the letter that reads something like, "Be sure to come up and introduce yourself to me next week. I really want to get to know you personally." This takes their acquaintance with you to a whole new level.

The Exciting Results of the Non-Glamorous Phone Call

Let's be honest here. Making phone calls to people you don't know personally probably isn't at the top of your "Exciting Things to Do" list. Yet through all my years in youth ministry I've learned that phone calls are one of the most valuable tools in creating a friendly atmosphere not just for your guests, but for everyone in the youth group. Shakespeare's King Lear said, "Nothing will come of nothing." And while all these different strategies for upping your "friendliness quota" require extra effort, please be one of the extraordinary people who choose a few specific ideas and put them into action. Did you realize that the term *work* appears in the

“Let's be honest here. Making phone calls to people you don't know personally probably isn't at the top of your 'Exciting Things to Do' list.”

Bible over five hundred times? Often, the answer to our prayer for a more friendly youth ministry is to simply get to work and implement a few of our good intentions.

It's best to call guests the evening following their first visit. Once again, you can delegate this responsibility to a couple of your student leaders. Try to select upper-level senior high students or college-aged adults to make the calls. If possible, have a male student call your male guests and a female student follow up on your females. To make this process easy to implement, consider having the person who makes copies of the guest information cards also make a second copy for the students making the phone calls. Then have a simple location near the copier where both your visitor letter volunteer and your phone call volunteers can easily pick up the information they need before leaving the youth meeting. Again, the more you can streamline the process, the more it will function effectively over the long haul.

> ### 60 Minutes
> "One way that helps me follow up on students is through something I call 'flock groups.' I hand out a list of names to our sponsors (adult volunteers) and ask them to take one hour a week to do some follow-up: fifteen minutes of making phone calls, fifteen minutes of writing letters, and thirty minutes of one-on-one time."
> —Matthew Nash, youth pastor in Robinson, Illinois

If you're a full-time youth leader or can spare an extra fifteen minutes a week, you might want to consider making these crucial guest phone calls yourself. But please beware: If you are one of the countless people who are more given to noble intentions than long haul follow-through, delegate this responsibility to a couple of teenagers without guilt. It is far more important to have the calls made consistently than to occasionally make them yourself.

The phone calls should be brief and upbeat. Train your teenage callers by demonstrating for them, in a positive tone of voice, something to say like, "Hi, this is Jeanne from Oxygen, the youth group you attended last night. I'm just calling to tell you again how glad we were to have you with us. " Warn the callers that the person may not respond positively, but that's OK. It's good to follow up with a question like, "We're really trying to effectively communicate with everybody who comes, and we'd like your help. Honestly, what did you think of the youth meeting?" Prep teenage callers to listen without being defensive or argumentative if the person has some negative feedback.

The call can be wrapped up with a warm invitation to return next week and with one simple question: "Without coming across as cheesy or anything, we at Oxygen really want to be a friend in any way possible. Is there anything I can do for you or remember to pray about?" Usually their answer is "no, thanks," but asking this question loudly communicates a positive message of authenticity.

Sometimes in my calls to visitors, they speak with pretty staggering degrees of honesty. I try to take notes and make sure that I really *do* pray about the situation—and not just promise to pray. Oftentimes when they later introduce themselves to me the following week, I try to quietly refer to their situation and let them know I had been praying. Time after time, I've seen light come on in teenagers' eyes with a knowing look that says, "Maybe these people are for real."

Expect the Grunts

As I mentioned earlier, ministering with personal phone calls isn't just for following up on visitors—it's also an important way to stay connected with the core students in your group. One of the top priorities in all of the youth ministries I've been privileged to lead has been giving adult leaders a list of students who they check up on briefly by phone every week. The students loved receiving these sincere calls! I trained my leaders to realize one important fact—most normal teenagers do little more than grunt over the phone. Without knowing this, even your best leaders will become discouraged and give up.

Allow me to relive the conversation all seasoned youth leaders have had over the phone. I regularly role-play this conversation for any adult volunteers who are helping me make phone calls so they don't think something is wrong with them.

> **Leader:** Hi, Ben. This is Dave Brickey from Oxygen. How are you doing?
> **Student:** Fine. *(Brief pause as the well-intentioned leader waits for more feedback. After seconds of deafening silence, the leader continues.)*
> **Leader:** Well, how'd your day go?

Student: *(In a grunting, bored voice tone)* OK.

Leader: What'd you do?

Student: *(Same grunting, bored voice tone)* Nothing.

Leader: Well, do you think I'll see you this week at Oxygen?

Student: *(Pausing, as though it's a challenging question)* Uhh…I don't know. What time does it start?

Leader: Oh, 7 p.m., Wednesday night. It would be great if you could show up.

Student: Well, maybe. I might be busy.

Leader: *(Pausing once again, hoping for more conversation while the other end remains quiet. Finally, the leader decides to wrap up the call.)* Well, Ben, thanks for letting me check in with you. If you show up tomorrow night, come around and say hi.

Student: OK. Talk to you later.

(The phone line goes abruptly dead, and the youth leader hangs up the phone, feeling like the president of the Losers of America Club. Inwardly he vows to lie about making his future phone calls and pray for forgiveness later.)

I've had hundreds of calls that sounded a whole lot like the one I just described. Having raised two sons myself, I've also been the listening parent on the other end of the call. Even my own boys acted like the typical teenage zombies when their volunteer small-group leaders called them. I can remember silently shaking my head, saying to myself, "No wonder my leaders don't always enjoy making their calls! This is about as motivating as watching paint dry!" However, when my young, noncommunicative teenagers hung up the phone, their mood took an obvious upswing! When they were in middle school, they would excitedly scream from the other room, "Hey Mom, Dave just called me!" As they reached high school, their "cool factor" took over, and no verbal comments were made, but it was obvious the phone call had made them feel great.

Weekly phone calls aren't glamorous, but they really make a huge impression. Today's teenagers may not be good at carrying conversations

> **"Weekly phone calls aren't glamorous, but they really make a huge impression."**

with people who are not their own age, but make no mistake: The phone calls are a big, big deal to them. No, they probably won't tell you personally until they're older—or they may *never* tell you. However, I promise that simple phone calls are essential to making your youth ministry feel more like a connected family.

The Data Proves It

I rarely like to believe something without seeing results. Of all Jesus' disciples, I think we all occasionally relate to doubting Thomas. I'm always silently thinking, "Prove it." Amidst my constant encouragement to my leaders to make the non-glamorous phone call, the doubting Thomas inside me wanted to prove to myself and others that phone calls really did work powerfully.

Not long ago, we did a survey among our own youth group. The survey was done randomly, using the approximately six hundred people who called our youth ministry "home." We enlisted other people to do the surveying so our influence would not cloud the results. We asked three questions:

1. How often do you attend Oxygen?
2. How would you rate your experience at Oxygen?
3. How often do you receive calls from someone in the leadership team at Oxygen?

The results were pretty convincing:

• On a scale of one to ten, 86 percent of those surveyed said their experience at Oxygen was an eight or above. Only one individual rated us a six. This helped me know that our focus to taking the actual service to a whole new level through friendship and creative communication had been successful.

• Of all the people called by a leader before the youth meeting that week,

83 percent of them showed up. That let me know that simple phone calls were effective in building weekly attendance.

- Though we didn't attempt to measure the emotional response to the calls in our survey, it was clear from the students' comments that they were positively influenced by the personal attention the weekly phone calls from adult leaders represented.

Other Strategies for Operation Follow-Up

Remember the Velcro points I described in Chapter 2? In order to heighten the friendship factor of your group, you need to work at creating Velcro-like sticking points for your new and fringe students. Here are some Velcro point follow-up ideas you can implement:

- Once a month we host "Dinner with Jeanne." I send a letter out to all our guests from that month, asking them to show up early for youth group the next week and have a thirty-minute dinner with me. I serve a light dinner (usually sub sandwiches, chips, dessert, and pop) and include a few key students and adult leaders who mingle with those attending, helping them to begin to feel more connected. Then I just share my heart with them for five minutes or so about how thrilled I am to have them coming around Oxygen. I casually open the floor for any questions. If the new kids don't ask any, some of our own kids bring up questions that typical newcomers might have.

As the month's guests leave our brief dinner together, I make sure I connect with each of them personally as they head into the youth group meeting. One second great result of this monthly dinner is that it's an easy way for some of our teenagers to be friendly to people they might

Balloon Bouquets

"Every Thursday afternoon, a team of students and leaders would head out to deliver a bouquet of balloons and a card to each of our first time guests from the night before. We rented a large helium tank and purchased foil balloons because they would hold air for two weeks. They cost a little more than the latex ones, but are a constant reminder floating around their room reminding them of their visit to our service. You can use generic balloons or spend a little more and get your logo printed on them."

—Dean Hawk, youth minister and youth ministry speaker in Colorado Springs, Colorado

> *"Teenagers really **want** to be friendly. They just lack the motivation and security to overcome their initial awkwardness with people they don't know."*

not normally talk with. Teenagers really *want* to be friendly. They just lack the motivation and security to overcome their initial awkwardness with people they don't know. So "Dinner with Jeanne" gave several of our kids a great way to get to know new people and perhaps begin a real friendship with them.

- Try "staking" your guests after they visit your youth service. We've found this tool to be especially effective with our middle school guests, though it works with high school kids too. We use the word *staking* because we create simple posters and attach stakes to them. After the youth meeting, we divide up the guest reception cards based on the part of town each kid lives in. Then a leader who lives nearby delivers the posters on stakes to the various homes at night. The poster says something like, "Thanks again, [first name], for showing up for Oxygen." These posters serve as an awesome encouragement when students see them as they leave for school in the morning.

- Host a focus group with guests who attend your youth group for a second or third time. Businesses use focus groups all of the time to gather customer feedback. In order to make our new students feel more quickly connected, we wanted to have a valid reason to ask them to return to Oxygen for a second or third time. Returning visitors were invited by phone to a fifteen minute focus group after the next week's youth group meeting to give some feedback on how we could make Oxygen more effective. We served snacks and included several regular attendees too.

This chapter has covered lots of specific follow-up ideas, but please don't try to implement every new idea this week! That holds the potential to cause a nervous breakdown. Even currently, I'm not attempting to do all of these at the same time. These are just a few great ways to up your friendship quota along your youth ministry journey. I've done them all and have seen positive fruit from each one. Though it takes extra effort to add a personal touch to follow-up, it's definitely *worth* it.

Now What? Ideas

Use these ideas to put the principles
in this chapter into action:

- Add all names of guests and their contact information into a youth ministry database.

- Write a short and inviting letter that you could send to your guests.

- If you do not have a secretary, target one or two key parents of teenagers in your group who could send out your guest letters each week.

- Think of four potential people who would be warm and friendly on the phone to make weekly guest phone calls. Invite these people to make phone calls, and train them how to do so.

- Consider doing an intensive six-week visitor survey to determine major strengths and weaknesses of your youth ministry.

- Get *Connexions: Postcards for Ministry* to have edgy postcards on hand when you'd like to send personal notes to students in your group. *Connexions* is available from Group Publishing, Inc.

_____

_____

_____

_____

_____

_____

_____

_____

_____

The Death of Mr. Clique

"That place is nothing but a bunch of cliques," the teenage girl I was meeting with said to me. I had just moved to a new youth ministry assignment, and I was meeting for coffee with a student who had decided to leave the youth group. She went on, "There's the in-crowd whose families have been at the church since Columbus came over on the ark. Then there's the kids who attend the Christian high school. Toward the back of the room, you'll find two more cliques. One is the row of home-school students, and the other is the small section of cool guys who spend most of the service smoking in the parking lot. If you don't fit into one of those cliques, you just don't fit in at all!"

She spoke with a direct, no-nonsense look in her eyes, and though I'd only been to the group for one week, somehow I knew that her analysis was pretty accurate. (Everything that is, except the minor confusion about Columbus coming over on an ark.) I met with several other students and asked them to give me their honest assessment, and I conducted an anonymous survey of the entire group. By evaluating the survey results and discussions with students, I became aware of two critical traits of our youth ministry:

1. Many of the students who were no longer attending the youth ministry—as well as about one-third of the current attendees—thought the
youth group was definitely cliquey.

2. The other two-thirds of the attendees, though not all Christians, were mostly
"good kids" and did not consider themselves to be cliquish or unfriendly.
While they agreed that sometimes the group could be cliquish, they were
each confident that the cliquish ones were a "they" and not a "we."

Why Cliques Exist in Today's Youth Culture

I began to sense that I was dealing with a slightly different social phe-
nomenon than what I had experienced fifteen or twenty years earlier in
youth ministry. I agreed with my "Columbus and the ark" friend that there
were definitely obvious cliques in the youth group. However, I was a little
surprised by how consistently open and warm many of the students were
with me when I talked with them one-on-one. I was also impressed with
how sincerely those I interviewed were against cliques and clearly didn't
consider themselves to be a part of one.

I asked God to give me insight to the root issue I was dealing with. It
didn't take much thought or prayer to have this reality surface: The root
of most unfriendliness and cliquish behavior in today's youth culture is
not self-centeredness or sinfulness. Rather, it primarily stems from students' personal awkwardness and insecurity when it comes to initiating
new friendships.

Please pause to think over that last statement. You may choose to dis-
agree, but I urge you to think long and hard about this conclusion before
you dismiss it. If it is correct, we need to rethink the way we deal with cliquishness in a youth ministry setting. Some youth leaders combat cliques by
delivering fiery youth talks about how bad cliquish behavior is—and they

*66The root of most unfriendliness and cliquish behavior
in today's youth culture is not self-centeredness or
sinfulness. Rather, it primarily stems from students'
personal awkwardness and insecurity when it comes
to initiating new friendships.99*

wind up blasting the whole youth ministry to pieces. While I'm all for challenging teenagers with a "no cliques" mantra, an effective approach must go a step further. If we truly believe that intentional friendship is a significant tool needed in youth ministry, we have to invest significant time in creating an atmosphere that makes initiating and cultivating friendships *feel natural*.

Why do teenagers today struggle with comfortably initiating friendships? One reason is that most of them have not grown up in healthy, functioning families with parents who have modeled the friendship process for them. Years ago, adults reached out to their next-door neighbors and others around them, building an extended network of friends. Unfortunately, this is no longer the case in most neighborhoods. It's become extremely rare for teenagers to see firsthand a "reach out to the neighbor next door" attitude. As a result, today's teenagers have heard more talk about friends than they have seen. The sitcom *Friends* ran for nearly a decade as one of this generation's most popular television series. Its overwhelming popularity highlights this generation's hunger for relationships. Even the obsession with "reality TV" is based on the idea of building relationships, yet ironically their "reality" is pretty slanted.

Secondly, think about the individuals your teenagers would call their best friends. They might name one or two, but who do they actually spend the most time with outside of school? The television or radio, most likely. This bombardment of media has given them an unrealistic perception of how to cultivate and create friendships. The plots they watch usually go something like this: Two people show up at a party or beautiful, park-like setting. Magically, they exchange names. They begin a little small talk, and then it happens. For some unknown reason, the two people decide

Loving the Lonely

"When I was a sophomore in high school, I attended a youth group and was pretty cynical. I knew I came across pretty hard, and I didn't expect them to care or accept me. Not only were they friendly and warm, but when I came back a second week, they remembered my name! Now, every week, I search out those girls who think they won't fit in and love them like a few amazing people did for me when I was a teenager. I know it's easier to gravitate toward kids who look like they have it all together, but breaking down social barriers has to start with our example as leaders."
—Cana Jenkins, youth worker in Sacramento, California

to take the plunge and exchange cell phone numbers. They cheerfully decide they'll "get together and hang out this weekend." After one or two evenings together, they begin a life-long friendship. Once in a while there's a third individual who the two meet at the gym or a coffee shop. Somehow, the whole get-to-know-each-other process begins all over again, and the trio becomes inseparable. It makes for a great story line in a movie or sitcom, but anything like this scene actually occurring between two teenagers who don't know each other is highly unlikely.

I once wrote this in my journal: "Unselfish love must be learned…and relearned…again and again." Unselfish love risks feeling like an idiot when the new person responds by grunting at you and making you feel like a loser. Unselfish love is highly intentional. It doesn't happen because a person is emotionally motivated to initiate it—and it sure won't happen because the music on the movie's soundtrack reaches a crescendo! As unglamorous as it sounds, intentional efforts to initiate friendships occur within a Christian context when we, as youth leaders, create a climate where friendship is emphasized, modeled, and made easy.

Through the years, I have witnessed a frightening reality. While the church has remained relatively disinterested and unintentional about creating an environment where positive friendships are easily cultivated, the enemy has not. Countless social environments exist in today's youth culture that make new friendships easy to come by. Just check out a few parties next weekend, and you'll understand what I mean. Technology has provided even more potentially unhealthy places for kids to meet, with chat rooms and other interactive Web sites. Unfortunately, many of those friendships are not Christ-centered. Repeatedly, students in our ministry hear me warn them, "Show me your friends, and I'll show you your future."

If one of God's promises to our students is an exciting, fulfilling future, we must concentrate on creating a youth ministry dedicated to building positive friendships. Our cliquish gatherings and holy huddles won't cut it. No matter how great your intentions are or how much you see the valid need for establishing this kind of Christian environment, it will never "just happen." You'll have to make this friendship focus on one of the core parts of your own heart and youth ministry efforts.

I know as a youth leader, and even as a parent, a holy huddle doesn't always sound like a bad idea. The problem is that in a clique, teenagers find a relational and spiritual comfort zone. When teenagers are stuck in a clique, they have a hard time talking to other people on a friendship level, hanging out with other people, and ultimately caring about other people. They stand off at a distance and only talk to the same three people at every youth group event. It's great that they have solid Christian friends, but in the long run, they become more and more their own island and engage less and less in the act of bridge-building.

Taking Aim at Mr. Clique

Most youth ministries, no matter how great they may be, are character-ized by small friendship circles that unknowingly make it difficult for oth-ers to feel included. How can you tell if your group has cliques? One way is to sit down one-on-one with students and ask them. I suggest you also take a night to stand back and just observe. Do the same three girls giggle in the corner every week and then rush out as soon as youth group is over? Do the same small circle of home-school kids sit by each other and quietly talk? How would a new person feel if he or she walked into the room? Would one of your teenagers immediately walk over and introduce them-selves? Make it your goal to help your teenagers look outside themselves and gain the confidence to be the kind of person who accepts everyone.

Remember the Paul Revere meeting and the S.I.P. I suggested earlier? Consider scanning through Chapter 2 again. Apart from putting into place workable strategies like these, your efforts to abolish cliquishness in your youth ministry will be disappointing and short-lived at best. Your sincere efforts to change the friendship culture of your group by merely preaching against cliques but not having an S.I.P. will probably not generate the kind of long-term change you desire. Your new strategies will make it much easier for normal teenagers to initiate and cultivate friendships in a Christ-honoring way. Teenagers, just like adults, are much more prone to repeat something if they feel successful. A wise youth leader makes it easy for teenagers in the group to successfully initiate new friendships.

Simple strategies, like having greeters at the door, hosting a guest reception, and using inclusive language will begin to reverse the tide of cliquishness in your group. Then, as I discuss in Chapter 9 (pages 129-139), you can implement a Point Guard ministry in which students act as row hosts and hostesses. Quite candidly, the row host and hostesses system requires little effort to launch. These suggestions are not tough to implement and have been road-tested. Then if you want to absolutely demolish Mr. Clique so he never rears his ugly head again in your youth ministry, take seriously the suggestions made in Chapter 6: "Small Groups Made Easy."

The Funeral

Ever had a funeral at a youth gathering? If you haven't hosted one yet, you might want to consider making it a priority in the next month or so. We did one not long ago, and it was one of the most energizing nights we've ever had. Granted, the funeral was pretty different from ones you may have attended, so let me explain.

I've learned that one of the greatest ways to communicate convicting truth without causing listeners to become defensive is through humor. That was our approach on the night we entitled "The Death of Mr. Clique." As the meeting started, here's how we set the scene: Somber, funeral music played in the background as we escorted teenagers (who were playing the family of the deceased) down the aisle. Each sobbed uncontrollably, and their wailing erupted in such a ridiculous way that the humor immediately began. They found their seats in the front, and then a well-dressed young man walked to center stage and stood piously with his Bible, acting as the minister for the funeral service. I strategically chose one of our most

"Teenagers, just like adults, are much more prone to repeat something if they feel successful. A wise youth leader makes it easy for teenagers in the group to successfully initiate new friendships."

gifted clowns for this important role; his very presence made the funeral scene a funny one.

Our minister solemnly greeted the small audience who had come. He spoke somberly, "We are here to honor one of our dearly beloved—someone who has played a vital role in our youth ministry up to this point. In reverence, the pallbearers will now enter with the casket of our esteemed deceased friend—our beloved Mr. Clique."

Six teenage pallbearers began down the aisle solemnly carrying a closed casket. A guest soloist sang a slow, unforgettable version of "Amazing Grace." We had rewritten the words to accommodate our theme, and she completed her appearance with a hysterical thrift store dress and flowered hat. She obnoxiously belted out, "Amazing cliques, how safe the sound that marks our youth group now. We once were warm to all God sent, but now to only our friends." We borrowed an inexpensive casket from a local funeral home and placed it in the front as the mourners continued to humorously add their own drama. One guy ran up from the family row, beating on the casket, yelling, "My beloved Mr. Clique! It's so lonely without you."

One key to the success of our funeral service was selecting fun students to participate—kids who are well-loved by others in your group and who are able to ad-lib. You'll love the results and so will your students!

Our funeral service progressed with the normal components. We had a couple of people share how Mr. Clique had made an impression on their lives. One individual talked about how she had always admired Mr. Clique and wanted so desperately to be a part of his elite circle. Another spoke about how life-changing it had been to be a part of this tight circle of four people who refused to let others get close to them. He hammed up his speech about how he felt his whole world was complete with his "four and no more." Instead of having another song at our funeral, we asked a few students to compose a rap in honor of Mr. Clique. As the

"Initiating new friendships is hard for all of us."

family sobbed and the eulogies rolled, our rappers broke into their own personal memorial.

The minister gave a five-minute message about Mr. Clique. He shared truth but did it in a voice tone that seemed complimentary instead of critical. "Here lies our beloved brother, Mr. Clique. He has been a part of this youth group for quite some time now. None of us are really quite sure when he came to reside among us, but his presence has been evident for months. Yes, who else could make it so difficult for new friends to start coming back to our youth service? I ask you, men and women, who else could have done that job so admirably for us? Who else could have created an atmosphere where even some of *us* felt slightly awkward when our close circle of friends would not be attending the evening service? We have our esteemed Mr. Clique to thank for this marvelous result. Yes, we owe it all to our friend and trendsetter, Mr. Clique. Mr. Clique has slowly but dramatically changed the atmosphere of our youth group on a weekly basis. Strangely enough, many of us were totally unaware of his presence among us, yet Mr. Clique has produced results that have been consistent, steady, and undeniable."

The content of your minister's message can take off in any direction. Our minister concluded his presentation by saying, "And so tonight, dearly beloved, we officially lay to rest Mr. Clique. He will no longer be among us at our weekly gatherings because we here at Oxygen are strategically launching a new mission of Christ-honoring friendliness around here. Do you hear me, brothers and sisters? Mr. Clique's dead tonight! Do I hear an "amen"? This brother, though a part of our company in times past, will no longer live among us. Ashes to ashes. Dust to dust. May God rest his self-centered soul."

After a humorous closing prayer, I got up and spoke for a few minutes about our new goal of making Oxygen one of the friendliest places in the city. I was careful not to preach at the teenagers or beat them over the head emotionally. My tone of voice wasn't negative—it was understanding. I let them know how I realized that initiating new friendships is hard for all of us.

I told them that I knew most of them wanted to reach out in friendship, to get to know other people, and to make everyone feel welcome each week. I told them that I knew many of them had friends at school who they'd love to invite to our youth gathering if they thought it was safe enough. I explained our new launch, complete with key things that would help our youth ministry begin to have a much more friendly atmosphere. I briefly touched on some of the pragmatics from our S.I.P. and then told them that I knew it took guts to reach out to others—that it was really tough for all of us to push pass the awkwardness. I reassured them that we were going to help make that easier.

I closed the night out with an anonymous poem called "My Friend." It spoke of a student who now was eternally condemned. The student had a close friend who knew about Jesus, but never shared. It ends with a line that basically asks: What kind of a friend would hide their faith, if they knew it would matter for all eternity?

I wanted the kids to understand the eternal reality at stake in this new friendship focus. Then I wrapped things up by saying, "Gang, I need your help. We're not asking you to walk away from your current circles of friends. We're just asking you to begin opening up those circles, at least on Wednesday evenings, by involving yourself in some of the simple changes we are going to start next week. But I can't do this by myself. I need all of you on my team. We promise to work hard to make this a place you can be proud to bring your friends to. With all the creative things we are hoping to implement, your friends will be most affected by your simple, authentic friendship."

I asked that every student who was willing to commit to changing the friendship environment of the group to stand up. I don't remember the music that started after that. I just remember the rumbling of chairs on the gym floor. The evening that had once started so comically, now became intensely serious. Slowly, over 95 percent of the students stood up. Before they left that night, I asked them to spend time talking with a couple of other people they didn't know. To someone standing in the back, it probably appeared to be just a bunch of rowdy kids talking to each other. But to me, it was the beginning of a social change, of a *tipping point*. It normally took just five to ten minutes for the students to leave after youth group ended. That night most lingered for over thirty minutes. That noisy chatter of teenagers earmarked one of our most crucial steps in the process toward building an environment of authentic friendship.

Keeping Mr. Clique Underground

In addition to hosting a funeral for Mr. Clique, consider implementing some of these strategies that will keep Mr. Clique's coffin deep underground.

1. Train yourself and other key leaders to intentionally use language that breaks down social barriers and makes everybody feel included. Here are some lines we regularly repeat:

   - "Here at Oxygen, we don't care if you're Catholic, Lutheran, Presbyterian, or Baptist. Around here, we're not into religion. We're into relationships."

   - "We all come from different backgrounds. Some of us attend Folsom. Others attend Rancho. Some of us come from families with a lot of money and others of us have to work to make ends meet. None of that matters. We believe the ground at the foot of the cross is level for everyone."

   - "Some of us are football heroes, and others of us are computer nerds. It doesn't matter if you're a prep, geek, jock, or nothing. We're just glad to have you! Christ died for all of us and sees us all as his kids."

   - "At Oxygen we're not as much a youth group as we are a youth family. And whether this is your first time here or your millionth, we're really glad to have you."

2. Target key influencers of different age groups to break down barriers. Granted, you've read those words "target key influencers" over and over, but it's key in creating a friendship climate. Remember the Pareto Principle— 20 percent of your efforts will create 80 percent of your results. With this in mind, you need to repeatedly realize that approximately 20 percent of your students establish the spiritual and emotional climate for 80 percent of the group. Jesus carefully selected his twelve disciples. He poured himself into those twelve men, believing they would change the world…and they did.

   If you want to break down cliques, determine who the "kingpins" are in the different demographic segments represented in your group. Sometimes it will be segments of racial division, monetary division, age-level division, or just social division. Talk privately one-on-one with the key individuals from each of these different pockets of influence. Share with them your desire to make sure everyone feels included in the youth group. Then bluntly ask for their help. Teenagers respond positively when we choose not to come across as the leader and instead humbly ask them to be on our team. Remember: What people are not up on, they're down on. Any true changes you want to make in the friendship climate of your youth ministry must begin when you make sure your key influencers are "up" on it.

3. Purposefully put kids from all different groups "up front" in your weekly meetings. Get them involved in making announcements, leading prayer, directing a game, performing a skit, or leading worship. The teenagers who consistently are in front of your youth group make an impression on participants, so make sure that in some capacity teenagers from different social groups and different ethnic backgrounds are represented. Work to avoid the trap of using the same students in up-front roles over and over again. I'm not suggesting you elevate the drug addict in the back row to the role of emcee, but I *am* suggesting that your back-row groupies need to see someone up front whom they relate to.

4. Verbally reinforce the new positive atmosphere. What gets rewarded, gets repeated. That simple statement is so true. That's why you have to train yourself to make frequent positive statements continually reaffirming the goal of an authentically welcoming environment. When you catch someone doing something good, point it out! Say things like,

> ### Find a Friend
> "We took our small group along with another to the mall for an outing. The teenagers had no idea what we were going to do. We'd asked a few of the 'cooler' ones from the group to dress up like homeless people—completely unrecognizable. The rest of the gang was instructed to find their friends (the dressed up ones). It took them nearly an hour! They all learned a lot about appearances, especially the ones who were dressed up 'lower' than their normal social status. They were treated horribly by other mall-goers. It helped them see that their clothes, their cars, and their social status were not all that important. And they got to walk in someone else's shoes for a day."
> —Jordan Marcon, youth worker in Atlanta, Georgia

"Your back-row groupies need to see someone up front whom they relate to."

"Dan and Suzanne are heroes around here because they so unselfishly reach out to others." Your affirmations do not always need specific names attached to them. Just begin to verbally affirm the group as a whole for reaching out to others.

In *The Friendship Factor,* Alan McGinnis details a study of a second-grade classroom in which discipline became a problem. The teacher was monitored by psychologists as she attempted to get the rowdy class under control. The researchers noted that the teacher told the students to sit down about seven times every twenty minutes—without much success. The teacher then began to increase her efforts to take charge of the classroom, telling the kids to sit down much more frequently—an average of 27.5 times in twenty minutes. Surprisingly, this increased and commanding vigilance had the opposite effect of what the teacher desired: The students became significantly more disobedient and rambunctious. Again, she further increased her efforts to command that students sit down and, of course, the students responded by ramping up their rowdy behavior.

Finally, the psychologists prompted the teacher to avoid commanding disobedient kids to sit down and instead to verbally affirm and encourage the students who were behaving well. The kids behaving poorly noticed the positive reinforcement they were missing out on, and they started to replicate the good behavior of their classmates. The results of the study showed that verbal affirmation produced the best student behavior of all the discipline approaches! The change in behavior came as a result of verbalizing and focusing on the positive rather than the negative.

I'm certainly not suggesting that we not clearly address negative forms of behavior. But sometimes as youth leaders, it is easy to forget that long-term change is created through authentic affirmation of positive behavior more than constant nagging against negative behavior. Remember the opening premise about becoming a youth ministry frog kisser? If you want Mr. Clique and all his relatives to be permanently put to death in your youth ministry, then make sure you verbally kiss some frogs when you're leading events and meetings and you'll begin to have more princes surface all around you.

Now What? Ideas

Use these ideas to put the principles
in this chapter into action:

- Consider hosting your own "Youth Ministry Funeral."

- Determine who you need "on your team"—key student influencers who are capable of making or breaking this friendship focus.

- Meet with those key influencers personally, and ask for their help in destroying cliques.

- Ask a few key students to observe you speaking for a few weeks, and make note of any sentences or phrases that might unknowingly create an impression that is not inclusive and open to different types of students.

- Make a list of specific phrases you'll start incorporating in your talks that make the atmosphere of the group feel truly accepting.

- Write down the names of three to five students who you've observed making an effort to be friendly and welcoming. Praise them for it!

- Build closer relationships with students in your group by using the programming ideas in *UnityBuilder Devotions for Small Groups* (Group Publishing, Inc.).

_____

_____

_____

_____

_____

_____

_____

_____

_____

Chapter 6

Small Groups Made Easy

I should have been smiling that night after our youth gathering concluded, but I wasn't. Our attendance had been high that evening, complete with more first-time guests than ever before. Yet my mind raced back to the discouraged single parent who had called my office late that Wednesday afternoon.

"My son doesn't want to come back to your youth service," she tried to explain over the phone, "and I'm begging you to do something to help, Jeanne." When her voice broke on the other end of the line, I knew I could not consider this call just business as usual. The desperate mom tried to get another sentence out, but the words stuck in her throat as she fought to hold back embarrassing sobs.

I heard myself utter, "I'm still here, Mrs. Harris. Don't feel you have to hurry. I really want to help." The next twenty seconds of silence felt like eternity from my end of the phone. I mentally clamped my lips, refusing to offer to this desperate single parent "TRT" (typical religious talk). Finally, she got enough control to finish the rest of her all-too-common story.

"Brian's dad left us for another woman about three months ago. Brian was never a very popular kid at school or anything, but this must have

> **"The larger the group became, the easier it was for nameless faces to attend and just slip through the cracks."**

pushed him over the edge. Last weekend, I found him passed out in his room. He had emptied my medicine cabinet and taken everything he could get his hands on. He told me later that he didn't have any friends and just didn't want to live anymore."

I knew that statistic all too well. In America today, almost every family is somehow affected by divorce. The percentages between divorced Christians and divorced non-Christians are frighteningly close. As far as attempted suicide, Brian was not an unusual case on that count either. Just a month or so earlier, I had rushed to Midland's Hospital where I watched another teenager's stomach be brutally pumped after an apparent suicide attempt. "Kind of rough, aren't you?" I remember questioning the emergency room doctor. He glared at me as he pushed the tube deeper into the teenage girl's throat and stomach. "The idea is to make this so unpleasant that she never wants to try it again," he mumbled back. The terror in the young girl's eyes that night, as she squeezed my hand, haunted me for weeks.

I came back to reality as I heard the single mom continue, "He says that no one at your youth group really wants to be his friend either. Apparently, only some kids occasionally say hi to him, but he feels like nobody remembers his name or wants to sit with him. I'm going to force him to attend one more time, tonight. Could you just please do something to make my son feel like he is more than another face in the crowd?"

I gave wholehearted assurances to this overwhelmed single mom that things would be different this week. I hung up the phone with her words still echoing in my head, "He says nobody remembers his name or wants to sit with him. Could you please do something to make my son feel like he is more than another face in the crowd?"

Granted, my answer for this young, troubled freshman in high school on that particular night came pretty easily. I called a couple of guys from the freshmen-age small group. Without breaking confidentiality, I told them enough of Brian's story so they would realize the urgency of their mission. "Guys, it's not enough to just give him a token hi tonight and then sit with your buddies. You've got to *own* him. I mean, chase him around the whole church if you need to. Make sure he sits with you two tonight and that you invite him to your small group." Before I hung up the phone with each of them, I paused for emphasis.

"Got it, Luke?" I said to one of them. "I need you to *own* him and *chase* him—not just tonight, but indefinitely. Make him feel like he has true friends in your small group." I started to hang up the phone, but I was still afraid the message hadn't gotten through all the way. So I punctuated my urgent message with nine more words: "Kind of like Brian's life could depend on it."

Owning, Chasing, and Family

I'm not really sure when the verbal terms, *owning, chasing,* and *family* became second nature in my youth leadership training. But now, thirty-five years later, they remain as common in my leadership vocabulary as *thee* and *thou* were for good 'ole King James. The problem was urgent: How many other Brians were out there who needed to feel a genuine sense of being owned, chased, and part of a family? The glamour of youth ministry growth was quickly losing its glitter as I realized that the larger the group became, the easier it was for nameless faces to attend and just slip through the cracks.

The term *chase* entered my ministry vocabulary after I read a poem by Francis Thompson called, "The Hound of Heaven." The poem depicts God relentlessly pursuing a relationship with the author. I stopped as I was reading that day and mumbled to the Lord, "That's what all the Brians of the youth culture need, Father. They need to be tenaciously *chased* with your love by people who are so persistent that they are like the very hounds of heaven." Yet, like a lot of things in youth ministry, it seemed far easier to *define* the problem than it was to fix it.

I tried to implement all the typical answers. I begged for adult and college-aged church members to be leaders within the weekly youth gathering. Then I divided up the students' names into separate groups the volunteers could focus on. But it seemed that these groups were little more than impersonal calling lists. I even tried to launch a full-blown small-group system within the youth group, whereby smaller groups met every week in homes. I remember returning from a leadership seminar that had pumped me up about the ease of launching these small groups. There was only one problem: All my good adult leaders looked at me like I had just grown two heads when I suggested they give up another night of the week to run these groups. The guy who conducted the seminar on small groups must have just had more committed leaders, I consoled myself.

In spite of it all, I knew we had to implement a small-group strategy that would own kids, chase kids, and make them feel like family. Mere telephone calls weren't working because the leaders and students needed to regularly see each other face to face in order for a sense of family to develop. But hosting a full-blown small-group ministry wasn't going to cut it either. It's pretty tough to divide your entire group into small groups when your leaders are all threatening a mutiny if they have to give up another night of their week.

So allow me to share with you a simple, workable plan for how to make small groups easy. Launching a simple form of small-group ministry will be one of the most important moves you can make in youth ministry. I've concluded that it's impossible to achieve maximum ministry effectiveness without them. I believe this truth applies whether your youth ministry is ten students or five hundred. Your small groups become a primary means for personal ownership, discipleship, and numerical growth. So go grab another cup of coffee, get comfortable, and allow me to walk you through some pragmatic steps that will impact the growth, retention, discipleship, and ministry impact of your youth ministry. Ready? Let's roll!

Find a model.

First decide on a workable small-group model that will best fit your group. This decision is strategic. There are countless small-group models and philosophies floating around today. I'm going to focus on the model that has worked best for us in my experience: hosting the small groups at the church, as a part of your youth meeting every four to six weeks.

I've found that to truly make small groups "easy," this model is best. There are countless aspects of this model that make it much easier to launch and sustain. First, it doesn't take another night of the week away from your leaders or students. Second, it doesn't require a high level of follow-up to ensure that people will be present. Third, leaders are able to run their small groups with less difficulty because you are helping plan the meetings and you launch the first part of the youth night for them.

During my tenure in youth ministry, all of my small-group ministries have eventually transitioned to being held on another night of the week and in people's homes. But they all were *launched* using the simple system I am about to explain. Here are the basics:

- Small groups are hosted only once every four to six weeks.

- The groups are hosted as a part of the regular youth meeting.

- Groups are assigned different areas of your meeting space in which they regularly meet together.

- On small-group breakout nights, everyone meets together first. The youth leader then introduces the discussion topic. It's best to use a brief drama to creatively whet the appetite of the students before dismissing groups.

- Leaders are given a sample game plan of what they will be doing with their students while in the small-group meetings. I've included an outline for a small-group session on pages 99-102 that you might want to use as you launch your small-group program. (Once adult leaders get the hang of it, they can start developing their own meeting plans.)

Common Interests, Common Goal

"Our small-group program consists of interest-based groups. One Wednesday night while walking out of a youth service, I noticed a group of young men standing around a car, freestyle rapping. They were our hip-hop cell group, but we weren't utilizing that avenue to minister to them. Now the hip-hop cell group meets on Friday nights and runs upwards of fifty people. We have groups whose emphasis ranges from basketball to photography, surfing, prayer, outreach, movies, and different hang-out groups. We have found that the kids are more willing to be involved in this ministry because they are doing so with people who share the same interests as themselves."

—Johnnie Wilson, youth pastor in Orlando, Florida

- Small-group leaders are encouraged to make phone contacts with their students throughout each week and host occasional small-group parties or events to help build relationships, fun, and a sense of belonging.

- Eventually, if the leaders want to, the small groups may transition into meeting in homes on a weekly or biweekly basis.

Create a list of "regulars."

Once you've decided on the format your emerging small-group system is going to use, begin to create a list of the regular attendees to your youth ministry meetings and events. Even if your group is a very small one, make sure you have an accurate database of student information. Have teenagers fill out information cards that include their name, address, phone number (including cell phone), age, grade, school, e-mail, birthday, and names of parents.

Draw up a list of "prospects."

Every church, large or small, has students "hiding in the wings." These are the students who, if reached out to in genuine friendship, could be easily drawn into the regular life of your youth ministry. Before reaching out evangelistically, it makes sense to first become a shepherd to the spiritual fish that are already laying around on your own dock. Let me list some of the places I draw from to develop our "Prospects" list:

- Request permission to make a brief, verbal announcement on Sunday morning during the main church service. Share enthusiastically that your youth group wants to reach out to include many other students.

> **"Every church, large or small, has students 'hiding in the wings.'"**

- Request leads from adults in the church. Ask them to give you information regarding any students in their family or friendship circles that they would like for someone to personally contact and invite to the youth gathering. You will be amazed at how much your stock will go up in the eyes of parents and grandparents when they see your sincere efforts to include some of their loved ones.

- Request your students' help in creating a list of teenagers who used to come to the youth group but have since dropped out.

- If your church has Sunday school for teenagers, check in with the Sunday school teachers, and get a list of all the students who attend. Many faithful attendees of Sunday morning programs have never been to a mid-week youth event.

- Scan current and past church directories to look for teenagers who have somehow slipped between the cracks.

Creating an accurate list of small-group prospects will take some time and energy on your part. But remember the parable in Matthew 18:10-14 where Jesus talked about the Shepherd who left the ninety-nine sheep in the fold to search out one little sheep who wasn't in the group? Jesus was relentless in his pursuit of people.

Step 4

Begin the process of adding and dividing.

Don't worry—it's simple math. Add the names you compiled from steps 2 and 3. Then divide the lists into groups of six to eight of your regular attendees (three to five if your ministry is smaller) and one to three names from the prospect list (depending on how long your list is).

I often divided up my tentative small-group list before I began to think of who might lead them. Usually, as I began this small-group approach, I lacked the necessary adult leaders to help me effectively reach out to all of these groups. Thus, the exercise of dividing our youth ministry into workable, smaller groups became a valuable catalyst that forced me into aggressive recruiting of potential leaders.

How should you divide up the kids? Here are some guidelines:

- Attempt to keep students together who are close in grade-level. Most importantly, separate middle school students from high school students. Young teenagers' lives and personalities are so very different from older high school students! By keeping students with those in a similar age-bracket, they'll be much more likely to open up and feel comfortable with each other. Some youth ministries also separate guys and girls into gender-specific groups. We usually have mixed-gender groups, but you may want to separate them if you aren't sure they're emotionally or spiritually mature enough to function as a "family" together.

- Try to put students together who attend the same school. Why? Because living close to each other and seeing each other regularly will allow natural friendship to develop more easily.

- Avoid placing too many social leaders into one particular small group. Anchor each group with at least a couple of students who you believe would carry some influence. It can be terribly defeating to a youth ministry if all the "cool kids" went to one or two groups and all the "un-cool kids" went to other groups. Teenagers quickly pick up on these signals, even when they're not purposefully sent.

- Separate any of your obvious "T-teams." That's my name for any groupings of two or three kids who, when together, have a way of creating *trouble*. You'll be encouraged to see how different personalities emerge when some of these students who negatively feed off each other are not in the same small group.

- When possible, give all of your students a minimum of one other student they already know and would genuinely *like* to be in a group with. The idea in forming small groups is certainly not to separate all the good friends from each other. Your groups will go better if some of those healthy friendships are left intact. Just make sure that unhealthy relationships are separated and that larger friendship circles do not comprise the bulk of an entire small group.

- Having divided your regular students into different groups, go back and supplement each list with some of your prospects. Try to place prospects in a group with students from similar grade levels and schools whenever possible. These names and phone numbers can become ground zero for your new leaders as they try to grow their emerging groups. The small-group leaders can commit to pray for these prospective students and begin personally inviting them to attend.

Some of you may feel discouraged at this point because your present youth ministry is so small that creating even two small groups is a stretch. I promise you this simple approach will monumentally help increase the friendship factor in your ministry and will help with numerical growth. Take heart! I came to faith in Christ in a youth ministry of about ten students, and it impacted my life in eternal ways. Never underestimate the importance of your ministry, at any size.

And remember: The effectiveness of your small groups will be in direct proportion to how much energy you spend in these opening steps of preparation. Groups that are quickly thrown together will often become groups

Natural Friendships, Natural Growth

"One of our failures pertaining to small groups has been in how we form them. When we first started utilizing a small-group structure, we thought it would be a great way for kids to get to know other kids they didn't know very well. So we divided our entire group up into small groups, purposely trying to group students with other students they may not have known very well. Great intention—bad idea. Of course our kids didn't like being stuck with people they didn't know very well, and as a result, true ministry didn't happen.

We realized it was more important for our kids to have a few strong, healthy, spiritually productive relationships with other students and leaders than for them to get to know everyone in our entire group better. Students need strong relationships in order to survive and thrive in their Christianity!"

—Bob Pankey, associate pastor in Whittington, Illinois

that will quickly fall apart. I can hear some of you thinking, "The title of this chapter, 'Small Groups Made Easy,' was a big joke, Jeanne. This doesn't sound *easy* at all to me."

Though organizing and launching one of these groups take some time, the actual fruit of them will be very easy to perpetuate. Once students are in small groups, ideally they will stay with those same groups until they graduate. Trust me on this one: You will be amazed to see the friendship, numerical growth, and spiritual fruit that will begin to emerge from your small groups.

Step 5

Recruit and place adult leaders.

If your current leadership team looks a lot like a deserted island, you are not alone! The most common cry I hear from youth leaders all across the country is, "I don't have any committed leaders." Take heart! On the other hand, if you *do* have some current, effective leaders, remind yourself to express sincere appreciation to them often. They are worth their weight in gold.

Current leaders need to be matched with your new groups according to their personalities. Every one of your new groups will need at least one adult leader who finds it pretty easy to connect with the teenagers. Avoid the temptation of making a well-intentioned adult the primary leader if he or she has a personality you know won't mix well with the average teenager.

If you need to recruit additional leaders to head up your small groups, here are a few tips to help you get started:

• Remember that great leaders come in all shapes, ages, and styles. Don't just limit yourself to young couples or cool college students. One of my greatest small-group leaders was a fun-loving grandmother named Peggy Bradbury who impacted the lives of countless teenagers.

• Focus on recruiting leaders one person at a time. Jesus didn't assemble his leadership team (the disciples) using church bulletin inserts or impassioned announcements from the pulpit. He personally recruited them.

• Ask potential leaders if they want to meet with you so you can share with them your passion and vision for the youth ministry.

• Meet informally with these potential leaders one-on-one. Share a meal or snack together, then take five to ten minutes to tell them about your excitement for the youth ministry and your vision for the new small-group ministry. Hand them several student information cards, and ask if they'd be willing to attend the youth group in an effort to reach out in friendship to the students named on the cards. It is easy to casually turn down requests to "help with our church's youth ministry." Your request for help will be much more effective when the potential volunteer looks at the cards and sees that his or her efforts will impact specific kids.

• Invite potential leaders to get involved in the youth ministry for a three-month trial period. In addition to attending the youth meetings, explain that you'd also like them to invest only thirty more minutes by making brief phone calls to each of their students on a weekly basis.

• Make it clear that you would be thrilled if they decided to stay on as a regular part of the leadership team after the three months ended, but that there is absolutely no obligation to do so. You are just asking them to partner with you and give youth ministry a try to see if this might be something they would really enjoy.

Why just three months? Many people are unavailable because they burned out during a previous ministry commitment that lasted too long. Picture the sincere guy who responded to a guilt-laden appeal for nursery workers. He signed up and fulfilled his commitment for the next year even though he hated almost every minute of it. He knew after two weeks the nursery wasn't his thing, but he was trapped in a year's commitment.

Lots of great potential volunteers will be happy to give youth ministry a try if you assure them they can resign without guilt if they desire to do so. Three months is long enough for them to catch the "youth ministry bug" if they're going to, but not so long that it feels like a never-ending commitment. You will be pleasantly surprised how many people will give youth ministry a try if they aren't scared of getting stuck there.

Invariably, leaders who begin to build strong relational ties *stay*. But if a leader does bow out after three months, comfort teenagers who became attached to the leader, and fill the position with another capable person. Consider combining two groups to keep things humming along smoothly.

“You will be amazed to see the friendship, numerical growth, and spiritual fruit that will begin to emerge from your small groups.”

Step 6

Double-check your group assignments.

After spending a month or more recruiting possible new leaders and deciding where you'd like to place your current leaders, finalize each small-group list. Each group needs to have one primary adult leader as well as a few student influencers. If you have enough adult leaders, you may see that you can assign assistant leaders to the groups as well.

Before announcing these groups to your students, run your lists by the adult leaders and two or three of your sharpest students. Ask them to keep the lists confidential, but request their feedback on any match-ups that might prove problematic. Often, the students help me greatly at this point. They'll say things like, "Jeanne, you don't want these two guys together. They'll drive a leader crazy!" or "This girl's personality is very dominant, so she needs to be with a strong adult leader."

Step 7

Establish a launch date.

Set a target date for when you are going to officially launch your small groups. Build momentum by mentioning it several consecutive weeks prior to your youth group meetings. The week before you officially launch your small groups, share a message that focuses on the importance of everyone feeling genuinely included. Enthusiastically explain your desire to have the youth group become a growing, thriving one in which everyone is a vital part of one of the emerging small groups. Stress to your gang, "Most of you will not be placed in groups with your closest friends. We're doing this because we already know each other really well. We want this youth group to be

Being proactive about letting kids know they aren't all grouped with their best friends will save you a world of problems when you later announce who is in each group.

really friendly, not cliquish. So thanks so much for being mature enough to not complain about the group you are placed in. We ask you to reach out and begin to help everyone in your group feel like family." Being proactive about letting kids know they aren't all grouped with their best friends will save you a world of problems when you later announce who is in each group.

Host a small-group leaders meeting.

Meet with your leaders to model for them what you want them to do during their small-group time. Plan carefully so it will be easy for even your relatively new leaders to pull off a successful night. Explain to your leadership team that they'll each be facilitating a small-group time during the regular youth group meeting once every four to six weeks.

Walk leaders through your small-group plan, using the sample small-group session I included on page 26, using a devotion you created yourself, or using a small-group resource. Encourage your small-group leaders to make changes and additions to the outline you provide for the night in order for them to feel a sense of ownership and to add some of their own personality. Eventually, your small-group leaders will know their students deeply and will be able to plan their small-group times on their own.

It's All Worth It

"Hosting a small group is no small task, but nothing could be more rewarding. The best things in life often require initial sacrifice, but no one who ever climbed the mountain regretted not staying at the bottom. Our goal was to create a place where teenagers could belong and feel important, knowing both security and significance. When we left our small group, they wrote us letters. I wept as I read the words of one quiet girl who we believed in and saw grow in a million ways. She confirmed to my heart that our goal was met. It made every sacrifice completely worth it.

She wrote: 'This was the first year that I ever felt included...I knew that someone really did love me...You made the insecure ones feel secure, making the excluded ones included. You loved me, spent time with me, and wanted to see me know God more. No one has ever done that for me before.'"

—Lesley Butcher, youth ministry volunteer in Edwardsville, Illinois

Clarify to leaders that the main reason you're implementing a small-group program is so that all the students will feel personally cared for and part of an authentic community. The *feeling* and *atmosphere* of the small-group time is just as important as the actual content of the discussion.

Create an awesome kickoff.

On the first night you launch the small groups, make all other ingredients of your youth meeting short in order to allow for the maximum amount of time possible in the groups. We usually start out with a short time of worship music and then a five to ten minute presentation on the topic the small groups will discuss. Before the groups are separated, be sure to create a positive atmosphere and family-like feeling. Set your leaders up for success before the students ever divide into their groups by positively asking the teenagers to make their group the very best.

It's up to you how you'd like to let kids know which group they're in. You may want to use PowerPoint, a handout, or simply call out their names. Be sure to positively reinforce the good attitudes you are attempting to cultivate. Play up-tempo music as groups are dismissed. If possible, have groups meet in the same area every week. Encourage leaders to bring beanbags or fun decorations. Let the adult leaders take over from there, leading their discussion time and dismissing their group at the end of the event.

Be there for the leaders.

Hang around after each small-group night to informally check with your leaders on how the night went. Celebrate their victories, and let them vent their frustrations. Your support will mean the world to them.

Plan ahead and keep your leaders informed by giving them a calendar that includes all the youth group meetings and highlights the small-group nights during which they'll lead a small-group discussion. Your organizational efforts will allow leaders to plan ahead—and will prevent feelings of burnout and fatigue.

10 Easy Steps to Launch Your Small-Group Ministry

1. Find a model.
2. Create a list of "regulars."
3. Draw up a list of "prospects."
4. Begin the process of adding and dividing.
5. Recruit and place adult leaders.
6. Double-check your group assignments.
7. Establish a launch date.
8. Host a small-group leaders meeting.
9. Create an awesome kickoff.
10. Be there for the leaders.

Stick With It

Part of "being there" for your leaders is not allowing yourself to quit when the normal bumpy times come. It will often take up to one full year to create a true small-group culture in your youth ministry. But the long-term dividends you will experience in your youth ministry's numerical and friendship growth will be well worth it. Remember the story I shared with you about Brian? I had called a couple of key guys in the freshmen small group and asked them to do their best to make him feel welcomed and loved. To tell the truth, I wasn't sure how things were going to work out.

It worked out in a way only God could have orchestrated. The young high school guys went out of their way to include Brian in their small group. Gradually, he began to talk freely with them because he felt like he had some genuine friends; his attendance at our youth group became not only consistent, but life-changing. A wise small-group leader even noticed some of Brian's natural abilities and began to affirm him in that direction. He gradually became a very trusted and responsible student leader in his small group.

When Brian graduated from high school, he chose to attend a local junior college so he could stay around and become the leader of a small group of incoming high school freshmen. Some of his buddies made fun of his decision to attend the less-than-glamorous junior college, but he just laughed them off. "If the small group I run can do for a couple of teenagers what my high school small group did for me, it will be well worth the sacrifices," he answered.

Years later, that once suicidal teenager is now a successful pastor in full-time ministry. Why? I believe creating small groups in our youth ministry began to "close the holes" in our spiritual net so that welcoming inclusiveness became a practical reality. Brian told me once that without the sense of belonging his small group brought to him, he believes he would have attempted suicide again. I'll never forget his sobering words, "And that time, I'm afraid I might have succeeded."

Small groups have played such a vital role in my years of youth ministry. They've given student leaders the opportunity to get involved. They've provided solid ways for teenagers to reach out within their comfort levels. They've provided acceptance and security for other Brians who might have otherwise chosen a scarier path. As you recruit leaders, divide up students, and begin the process, remember that Jesus is smiling, and your teenagers are worth it!

Got More Questions?

If you've launched your small-group program and questions have come up, check out the appendix on pages 141-143 where you'll find my answers to some of the most frequently asked questions about small groups.

Now What? Ideas

Use these ideas to put the principles
in this chapter into action:

- List the names of three to five Christians who have influenced your own spiritual growth. How did their friendship spur you on in faith? How can you replicate that aspect of Christian community for your teenagers?

- Identify some college students or adults who might serve as leaders.

- Host another Paul Revere meeting with these individuals to mobilize them for possible small-group leadership.

- Prayerfully, thoughtfully, and strategically divide up all your core students, making sure your key influencers are evenly spread throughout the small groups.

- Create an entire service to introduce and motivate your students toward your upcoming small-group launch.

- The following week, launch your first small-group experience, following some of the suggestions given in this chapter.

- Use the small-group meeting outline following this chapter (pages 99-102) to launch your small-group program.

- Get more small-group resources from my Web site, www.youthsource.com or at Group Publishing, Inc. (www.group.com).

- Learn more about developing your team of adult leaders by reading *No More Lone Rangers* by David Chow (Group Publishing, Inc.).

- As you dive into your small-group program, questions may come up. Check out the "Small Groups FAQ" section at the back of this book (pages 141-143) for more tips and insights.

_____

_____

_____

Small-Group Game Plan

Legacy

Use this meeting outline to launch
your small-group program.

For the Youth Pastor

PREPARATION

Recruit several students to create a "human video" to the song "Legacy"
from Nichole Nordeman's CD *Woven & Spun.* As the song plays, they should
pantomime scenarios in which teenagers reach out to other students, inviting them to join their small groups and then creating new "legacies" through
these Christ-honoring relationships. Make sure the human video team practices several times!

SUPPLIES

Make sure *each* small-group leader has a CD player (with batteries), a CD
of Christian music, the *Woven & Spun* CD, bookmarks with the words "Live a
Legacy" printed on them (one per student), photocopies of the "My Legacy"
page (p. 102), pens or pencils, and snacks for the students.

MEETING OUTLINE

• Begin your meeting with the entire youth group gathered together. Start
  out with praise and worship time, then take five to ten minutes to explain
  why you're launching a small-group program. Tell kids how it will work, and
  encourage them to view it as an opportunity to grow closer to each other
  and to Jesus. Challenge students to consider how they can use small groups
  to make an impact on others' lives. Use Scripture to teach about the importance of living a legacy of Christian love.

• Have the human video team perform their "Legacy" pantomime.

• Dismiss small groups to their meeting areas, and let the small-group leaders
  take over from there.

Small-Group Game Plan

Legacy

For the Small-Group Leader

REMEMBER...

- Thanks for being willing to invest in students' lives. You're incredible!

- Use this as a rough outline—feel free to add your own personality to the small-group meeting. Familiarize yourself with this outline ahead of time so you feel confident and comfortable.

- Be sure you know where your group will meet.

- If you're able, you might want to come early and decorate your meeting area to make it warm, casual, and inviting. Beanbags, pillows, or even a small rug will add to the home-like feel.

- Make sure you have all needed supplies.

- Your biggest assignment for the whole evening: Be friendly, friendly, friendly! Act as a "thermostat" instead of a "thermometer." Remember the difference? A thermostat *controls the temperature* of a room. A thermometer only *reflects it*. So control and create a climate of warmth, fun, and friendship even if it feels awkward.

- When your small-group time wraps up, take time to hang out with students—that relationship-building time is really important. Consider asking a few of your students to help clean up your meeting area.

SUPPLIES:
You'll need...

- ◯ CD player (with batteries, in case you're not near an outlet)
- ◯ CD of Christian music
- ◯ Nichole Nordeman CD *Woven & Spun*
- ◯ bookmarks with the words "Live a Legacy" printed on them (one per student)
- ◯ photocopies of the "My Legacy" page (one per student)
- ◯ pens or pencils
- ◯ snacks to share with your group

(continued)

TO START OUT...

Introduce yourself and welcome everyone. Have kids grab some snacks, then invite them to introduce themselves by telling about one person in their lives who has had a big impact on them.

DIVE IN...

SAY: **We're going to start playing the song they used in the human video and share with each other on a deeper level. All of us, whether we're fifteen years old or fifty, want to feel that we created some sort of authentic legacy; that our lives counted for something. And that's really a lot of what this small group is going to be about.**

Play the song "Legacy" on repeat throughout the rest of the small-group time. Pass out the "My Legacy" sheets and pens or pencils and explain that you'd like students to write their honest answers to the questions. Let them know that they should *not* include their name—their answers will be totally anonymous. Also let them know that you will read their answers aloud at the end.

Give youth five to ten minutes to write, then collect their sheets, mix them up, and read the answers aloud. First read all of the answers to question 1, then read aloud the answers to question 2.

Genuinely express your appreciation for everyone's honesty. Invite students to share any additional thoughts or ideas on the questions you've discussed. Talk about what a great start you're off to as a small group and let them know the date of your next small-group meeting.

WRAP THINGS UP...

Invite the group to stand in a circle, hold hands, and pray aloud by going around the circle. Ask students to each pray just one or two sentences, asking God to make the small group something really special. Let them know that if they don't want to pray aloud, they should just squeeze the next person's hand.

> **Tip:** Remember not to feel hurt if they are not too talkative yet. Some groups open up quickly. Others take a little more time. Whatever the case, just know Jesus is smiling as you begin this exciting chapter in your spiritual journey. You are beginning to write a legacy in the hearts of the students in your small group.

After the prayer, pass out the "Live a Legacy" bookmarks to the students as reminders of the night's discussion. Encourage everyone to hang out and play some up-tempo songs on the CD player. Walk around and mingle with the kids.

My Legacy

1. "I hear all this talk about this small group gradually becoming a family and an authentic group of friends, but sometimes words are cheap. If the people in this group really became genuine friends to me, I would need them to be people in my life who..."

_____

_____

_____

(Maybe you'd say something like...

• People who did some fun stuff with me. I just don't have a lot of fun Christian friends that I enjoy spending time with.

• People who accept me for who I am.

• Friends who really listen and actually care when I talk.)

2. "The idea of creating a legacy and having my life count for something eternal sounds pretty cool to me. But one of the main things that seems to stand in my way is..."

_____

_____

_____

(Maybe you'd say something like...

• Guilt over a bunch of the stuff I've done.

• The feeling that I can never measure up.

• I don't know if I really believe this God and Jesus stuff.

• Some painful junk that happened in my past. I laugh on the outside, but I'm really not laughing on the inside.)

Chapter 7

{It's all about a personal connection.}

Jeanne

What Youth Ministries Can Learn From the Business World

Imagine walking into a restaurant and no one acknowledging your presence there. Imagine going to a store and not being asked if you need assistance. Imagine walking into any business that provides a service and no one even approaching with a simple, "May I help you?" Pretty unlikely picture, don't you think? (At least for a place that wants to stay in business.) If the truth were known, most of us get pretty frustrated with poor customer service when we receive it in our personal lives. We often silently vow to ourselves, "I'm not coming back here again."

Though we all relate to these frustrations in the marketplace, they have huge lessons to teach us in the world of youth ministry. You see, the corporate world has spent billions of dollars trying to learn how to maximize their market and excel at customer service. We in the church believe we represent the most valuable "product" of all history: an eternal relationship with Jesus Christ. Yet our casual and often sloppy way of responding to our "customers" (teenagers) does not mirror the value of our "product." So what do corporate superstars like Starbucks, Disney, and Nordstrom have to teach us? Plenty. Let's jump in.

Disney Wow

A couple with a young kindergarten daughter took their vacation one year at the legendary amusement park Disney World. The little girl left her teddy bear and doll in the Disney hotel room as she excitedly raced off to the Magic Kingdom for her first day of vacation. When the family returned to their room that night, they found something more than a spotlessly cleaned hotel room. The maid had carefully positioned the treasured teddy bear and doll at a table as though they were eating. In the center, the Disney maid left a plate of chocolate chip cookies, obviously to be eaten by the teddy bear, doll, and their ecstatic owner.

At the conclusion of the family's second day at Disney, the little girl couldn't wait to arrive back at the hotel and see if the maid had left any other "Disney magic." Sure enough, this time they found the bear and the doll propped up in bed reading a Disney storybook and holding some fresh-cut flowers.

This isn't your average hotel experience. Perhaps this aspect of excellence in customer service could be summed up best by Michael D. Basch, CEO of FedEx, who wrote, "Legendary stories encourage legendary behavior." I bet that family became one of Disney World's best commercials in the years that followed this vacation.

What does it mean to have a "Disney attitude" in youth ministry? It means to go the extra mile in youth ministry "customer service"—to provide the extra "Wow!" that makes a big difference. Let me translate this idea into an example from real-life youth ministry. One Wednesday night in February, at the end of a youth meeting, I stood at the door and handed all the girls a fresh red carnation as they left. You see, Valentine's Day was coming up, and it felt like a great time to do a message I called "What Janet Jackson Never Told You About Romance." (Janet had just completed her historic half-time appearance at the 2004 Super Bowl, complete with her disrobing "wardrobe malfunction"!) As I prepared for the message, I realized many of the girls in our youth ministry were going to have a less than exciting Valentine's Day. So my little gesture at the door was a small touch of "customer service" from me that night. We didn't have money in the budget, so I bought the flowers myself. It may seem cheesy, but the looks in some of the girls' eyes let me know I was showing them Jesus' love in a big way that night.

66No matter how life-changing our 'product' is, we have the awesome responsibility of working hard to create a culture where teenagers are treated with respect, love, and responsiveness.99

What is "customer service" when it comes to youth ministry? It's realizing that no matter how life-changing our "product" is, we have the awesome responsibility of working hard to create a culture where teenagers are treated with respect, love, and responsiveness. They aren't treated like punk kids or spiritual convicts. Instead, we treat them as guests—as family—as people we sincerely want to return and become committed to our "product": wholehearted Christianity. I read the prologue to *Pour Your Heart Into It,* a marketing book that challenges businesses to move beyond half-heartedness. This quote jumped off the page at me as a perfect message for 21st century youth ministry:

> "Care more than others think wise. Risk more than others think safe. Dream more than others think practical. Expect more than others think possible."—Howard Schultz, Chairman and CEO of Starbucks Coffee Company, *Pour Your Heart Into It*

Nordstrom's Legendary Customer Service

Long ago, companies thought that a good product simply sold itself. (Unfortunately, many youth ministries are still stuck in this paradigm.) Then decades later, the buzz line in customer service became "The customer is always right." But today's philosophy of customer service has a new focus that we in the youth ministry world need to listen to. Put simply, that philosophy is that quality customer service is first and foremost *relational.* There are countless heralded stories from the corporate world that exemplify this focus. Let me share a few that have obvious implications to our youth ministries.

Many people recognize Nordstrom as the apex in department store shopping and personal service. One day, a customer returned a set of car tires to Nordstrom and demanded a full refund. The clerk questioned the individual regarding the purchase of the tires, but the person persisted that he had acquired the tires there. The clerk then smilingly returned the customer's tire money. The only problem? Nordstrom doesn't even sell tires! What is the implication for youth ministry? How many students do we alienate because we insist on our right to be right, even if it means the loss of a relationship? Maybe we would have stronger youth ministries if we did a better job choosing our battles in our efforts to *build* a strong youth ministry.

I recall another story about a man on his way to the airport for a golf trip with a prominent business client. On route to the airport, the client called and said that something serious had come up and that instead of golf, the two of them would need to appear at an emergency board meeting. The problem? Golf clothes wouldn't do for a board meeting with executives. As the man ran toward the airline gate, he called Nordstrom for help. Unbelievably, when he landed at his destination's airport, a Nordstrom employee was waiting for him with a complete outfit ready to go. After a short stop in the men's room to change, our would-be golfer was ready for his high-powered business meeting. What's the implication for youth ministry? Exceptional students are hugely impacted when we occasionally pay exceptional personal prices to serve them—especially when their backs are against the wall. (I can't tell you how many times I've helped teenage guys write moving apology letters to their girlfriends after they've blown it and lost the girl. Granted, helping undo romantic messes was never part of my job description, but two guys who are in full-time ministry today would tell you that my "customer service" in that arena many years ago was a turning point for them!)

Focus on Personal Attention

Howard Schultz, chairman and CEO of Starbucks and author of *Pour Your Heart Into It,* also has a message applicable to youth ministry. It seemed appropriate that I should reference Starbucks in this chapter because I just made my daily pilgrimage to my place of "early morning worship." It's a funny thing, but I pass several coffee shops on my way to the home of the circular, green logo. Yet, I'm a loyalist, enthusiastic about my fat-free latte and sugar-free vanilla (I prefer to spend my calories where they count like chocolate chip cookie dough ice cream). At any rate, the subtitle of Schultz's book might help to explain my unreasonable devotion. It boldly reads, "How Starbucks Built a Company One Cup at a Time."

What a riveting statement! And after thirty-five years in youth ministry, that same focus on personal attention is key to how the Lord has allowed us to build thriving and growing youth ministries, *one student at a time.* Granted, one leader cannot begin to do it alone. Your focus on personal attention has to be reproduced slowly into others, one leader and one student at a time.

So as I'm typing the manuscript for this book, sipping my Starbucks to get a caffeine jump-start, I see further evidence of Starbucks' focus on personal marketing. You see, my Starbucks cup is now staring at me with the name "Jeanne" neatly printed around its top. It's funny. I've never stopped to think about the significance of that move. But my favorite local Starbucks has a policy of writing the customer's name right on the cup so the barista can call it out personally when each drink is ready.

What is the implication for building a thriving youth ministry? There is no word in a teenager's vocabulary more enjoyed than the sound of his or her own name. As a matter of fact, we're modeling our youth ministry around a leader who "calls his own sheep by name" (John 10:3). I guess Starbucks wasn't the first to understand the importance of personal connection.

> **"There is no word in a teenager's vocabulary more enjoyed than the sound of his or her own name."**

When It Comes to Volunteers, Love 'Em or Lose 'Em

It's been called the best-selling employee retention book in the world, namely, *Love 'Em or Lose 'Em* by Beverly L. Kaye and Sharon Jordan-Evans. What does employee retention have to do with youth ministry? More than you probably think. The title itself gets to the heart of the matter. You see, thriving youth ministries are built around indispensable volunteer teams. People are not paid to give up their private time and show up to be a leader in your youth ministry. If you ever want to have other people helping you as a part of a leadership team, you would be wise to school yourself on showing appreciation to those working in the trenches with you.

The principle "Love 'em or lose 'em" means it is critical that you effectively take care of people on your leadership team. Without that team, your ministry will be significantly less effective. Tonight we're hosting a chili dinner at one of our leaders' homes. Hours before the actual gathering, I am experiencing the normal leadership frustrations: Leaders often complain that, "We never do anything socially together," yet when something is finally planned, the phone rings off the hook with people making last-minute excuses for why they "just can't make it." Such is the case this afternoon. Five of us may be eating a whole lot of chili tonight!

But begrudging as I am right now, I know the importance of hosting occasional get-togethers like this to make people on our youth staff feel like important members of a family rather than mere hired servants. So I'll go tonight and focus on the people who show up, sincerely trying to make them know how much I appreciate not only their ministry but their friendship.

In addition to getting together for meals and fun events, here are a few principles for loving your adult leaders:

- Consistently express appreciation—both in public settings and in private ones.

- Regularly take three extra minutes to call one of them out of the blue and tell them personally something positive you appreciate about them.

- Refer to them with honor in front of the youth group, using a title that communicates value and authority. I use *youth staff* rather than names like helper, sponsor, or volunteer.

- Host an annual weekend leadership retreat. Make it a refreshing weekend with training, encouragement, and motivation to help them keep focused on their important mission.

- Ask for the leaders' opinions and feedback. This will help them feel like it is their ministry, not just yours.

- Take a personal interest in the leaders' lives. Like most of you, I'm very busy and don't really have time for an extra meeting. But tomorrow morning, I'll be going out for breakfast with one of our leaders because I can tell she needs a friend now in a significant way. So I'll lose a couple of hours of sleep and meet her before she heads to her job. Remember that before you can really ask someone to buy into your *vision,* you need to buy into *them.*

- Recognize, celebrate, and reward volunteers' work. About six weeks ago, I unexpectedly passed out party hats, horns, and food in our leadership meeting. My reason? I told them we were "throwing a party to celebrate you!" You see, they had all worked really hard together on some youth ministry projects, and I wanted them to know that all their sacrifice had been noticed and appreciated. Schultz sums it up best in *Pour Your Heart Into It,* with one of his chapter titles: "People Are Not a Line Item."

> ### The Best Marketing: Word of Mouth
> "Our best method of marketing and promotion is our students. We pass the vision on to them, arm them with 3x5 cards we've printed with info, and send them into their schools. Nothing reaches students like students."
> —Brent Parsley, youth worker in Colorado Springs, Colorado

Go From Good to Great!

There are few business books that have challenged me in youth ministry as much as the best-selling business book entitled, *Good to Great,* by Jim Collins. The premise of the book comes from studying ten companies that made the leap from being good companies to great companies. I strongly recommend you read the book and gather wisdom for how you can make a good to great transformation in your youth ministry. If you're not into reading the entire book, just study the chapter summaries. They'll help you pick up on the primary principles and see obvious parallels in youth ministry. One of Collins' principles has made a big impact on me.

He tells of a conversation he had with Admiral Jim Stockdale, a former prisoner of war during the Vietnam War. Stockdale, along with other captured American soldiers, endured severe torture while imprisoned.

Stockdale explained that, sadly, the prisoners of war who refused to look at the blunt and horrible reality of the situation and instead fixated on overly optimistic dreams were the ones who weren't able to survive the torture and terrible conditions. Stockdale explained that a key to making it out alive was understanding and accepting that horrible reality while also holding on to the hope of being released. Only through that life-giving mixture of hope and realism could one find the necessary courage to endure the unspeakable hardships.

The Stockdale Paradox in *Good to Great* is summarized as: "Retain faith that you will prevail in the end, regardless of the difficulties." And at the same time, "Confront the most brutal facts of your current reality, whatever they might be." What life-impacting wisdom and encouragement for all of us in youth ministry!

If we are going to make the leap from being good to great with teenagers, we have to retain our faith that we will, by the power of Christ, eventually be more than conquerors. Yet along the youth ministry journey, we have to confront the brutal facts and realize that effective youth leadership calls for seasons of endurance and courage.

"Product" Feedback

The corporate business world knows another fact that we in youth ministry would be wise to glean from: It costs the organization far more financially to *gain* a new customer than it does to *retain* a present one. Every good public relations executive recognizes the importance of gaining new customers—but even more strategic, they know the importance of keeping current customers happy. As leaders of contemporary youth ministries, we all know the importance of the Great Commission (i.e. reaching out for "new customers") as well as taking appropriate care of our "returning customers" (our core students). But sometimes we have a tough time putting authentic feedback systems in place so we can find out how we're *really* doing.

How is that possible? First of all, it takes keeping channels of communication open between you and your customers (teenagers) and your employees

> *"Yet along the youth ministry journey, we have to confront the brutal facts and realize that effective youth leadership calls for seasons of endurance and courage."*

(leaders). I know, I know. You're probably thinking, "My leaders feel like they can come and talk to me, and the teenagers know my door is always open to them." I'm sure *you* perceive it to be that way, but sometimes, unknowingly, we have sent them other signals. Do you make teenagers or leaders pay emotionally when they try to make suggestions to you? Do you shoot down their ideas quickly or become a little defensive when they try to suggest change? If you don't like an idea, do you sometimes make its bearer feel silly or stupid? If so, you are probably not going to get much authentic feedback. Students and leaders will just silently begin to disappear or lose interest. At best, they will continue coming, but they certainly won't be a positive "advertisement" for your youth ministry.

Feedback experts know that if you're not hearing your customer's comments and suggestions, someone else is. As a youth leader, it took time for me to be brave enough to frequently ask for honest feedback. Human nature just enjoys hearing "How Great Thou Art" much more than honest critiquing! But continually and nondefensively asking, "How can we get better?" has been one of the biggest keys I've found to building significant youth ministries through the years. Proverbs 9:8 points out that a wise person loves rebuke. I've probably still got some growing to do before I reach the loving rebuke stage. But I do sincerely love the progress and growth it brings.

What can you do to begin creating avenues for feedback in your youth ministry? There are many ways to start. Here are a few suggestions:

- Host a few "Talk to Me" meetings (see Chapter 2). Invite some sharp students to critique your youth group meetings and events. Ask them to be honest, and force yourself not to explain or defend—just to listen. Take notes and make some changes.

- Every six months, provide your volunteer leaders with a form to give you feedback on the strengths and weaknesses of the youth group meetings. If you are really brave, also ask them for feedback on your communication style. Invite them to first give you some positive feedback. (Trust me. None of us is emotionally strong enough to handle the critiques without first knowing what we're doing *right*.) Then ask them to be specific and share suggestions for improvement. I usually have leaders do this anonymously, knowing that some leaders will be hesitant to give me good feedback if their names are included. Also invite leaders to write some dreams and ideas for the future. It's amazing how their creativity and visionary thinking will shape your youth ministry.

• Recruit students to be your eyes and ears, and ask them to give you an accurate report on the state of the youth ministry. I'm not advocating asking them to *spy* on their friends—but do invite them to honestly answer the questions, "What do you think?" and "How could we do this better?" The bottom line of our youth ministry has far higher stakes than the most prosperous Fortune 500 company. So getting honest feedback is a must.

First-Time "Customers"

Thriving youth ministries have learned to prioritize looking at their youth group meetings through the eyes of a first-time guest. Feedback from this vital group of people is an absolute necessity, especially if you want to be more than a weekly social club for the same returning group of students.

Martin Sklar, the vice chairman of Walt Disney Imagineering, created ten principles that reflect the values of Disney's founder, Walt Disney. Here are the first two of "Mickey's Ten Commandments":

1. *Know your audience.* Before creating a setting, understand who will be visiting or using it.

2. *Wear your guest's shoes.* Evaluate your setting from the customer's perspective by experiencing it as a customer.

(Excerpted from *Service Magic* by Ron Zemke and Chip Bell)

So having read the first two of "Mickey's Commandments," how are you doing? How intentional are you in your youth ministry when it comes to knowing your audience and wearing your first-time guest's shoes? Let me touch on a few areas that are impacting to those guests:

- *Create an environment that, in business terms, makes for an "easy sell" with new customers.* The music, the colors, and the design are all taken into consideration when people create a store or restaurant. Marketers, designers, and professionals are paid large amounts of money to decorate and create an environment that makes it hard for a customer to say no.

How can you create an inviting and multisensory environment for your youth ministry? First, begin with a vision; define clearly what you want your first-time visitors to experience. Second, adapt your "product" to your target market; stay relevant to teenagers and focus your energies on capturing their attention. Third, realize that everything you do sets the stage; each aspect of what you incorporate in your youth service helps establish an ambiance. Finally, evaluate your youth group meeting through some of the five senses. Ask yourself, "What will teenagers see, feel, and hear when they walk in the doors?" Just by answering those simple questions, you'll be well on your way to brainstorming and transforming your weekly gatherings with your strategic first-time guests in mind.

Over the years, we've worked tirelessly to create a cool and welcoming environment, often on a shoestring budget. We found that hanging used floor lights, black paint on the walls, a cool graphic on a backdrop, and dyed sheets used as curtains can transform a regular meeting room into an *experience.* Just involve the students to help decorate and you'll be amazed at the transformation in the look of your room.

- *Host focus groups for visitors.* As mentioned in Chapter 2, this once-a-month meeting is a way to nondefensively ask the month's newcomers, "What did you think? How can we get better?" You will glean a ton of helpful (and sometimes painful) insights on how you come across to guests. I'm not advising you to "water down" your Christian message to appeal to non-Christian visitors. But I am strongly suggesting that since Christ died for those people, we need to take reaching them very seriously.

Above All Else, Believe Deeply in Your "Product"

Pour Your Heart Into It captures the bottom line in youth ministry. Schultz believed that he had found his destiny after encountering a small, coffee bean producer from Seattle named Starbucks. In his book about how he became a part of Starbucks, he describes sitting on an airplane, feeling drawn to Starbucks. He writes, "There was something magic about it, a passion and authenticity I had never experienced in business. Maybe, just maybe, I could be a part of that magic." Schultz became enveloped in the coffee bean business and impassioned with its worth. Reading about his coffee "conversion" sounds strangely like the testimony of someone coming to life-changing faith in Christ.

The implications are clear for us in youth ministry. We have the greatest cause in the universe: that of the Gospel of Jesus Christ. Indeed, life becomes worth living when we find a cause worthy of giving ourselves to. How convicting it is to me personally that today's business world is often much more impassioned about their causes (coffee, amusement parks, clothing, and so on) than we are about the ultimate Cause of the universe.

Above all, I believe one of the greatest lessons that can be learned from extraordinary companies like Starbucks and Disney is their passion for their product. Starbucks sells coffee, and they believe it is for everyone. Disney sells entertainment, and they believe in entertaining everyone worldwide. How much more passionate should we be about the Gospel? Like the corporate executives, are we lying awake at night wondering how to strategically reach the youth of our culture? Do we stare out of airplanes, dreaming up new ways to be more effective? Or sadly enough, are most youth ministries simply content to survive?

The stakes are eternally high if we turn a deaf ear to our current and potential "customers." If our youth ministries are not growing, do we have enough courage to ask the hard questions and find out why? If MTV was not making progress in reaching the youth culture, they would be asking "why?" But in youth ministry circles, we often pretend that our lack of progress is due only to spiritual factors beyond our control. How agonizing—but how true.

Now What? Ideas

Use these ideas to put the principles in this chapter into action:

- Write or visit a few key, successful businesses that target youth in your area (such as a cool restaurant, skate shop, or clothing store) and pay attention to

  Ambience

  Appeal

  Customer Service

  Take notes, grab on to new ideas, and apply them to your youth ministry.

- Interview a few of your key students, and ask them where they hang out and why they go there.

- Choose a few students from different social groups to evaluate your youth ministry's "customer service."

- Decide on a few ideas that you will implement in your youth ministry to enhance "customer satisfaction."

- Come up with one idea for creating an inviting atmosphere in your youth ministry for each of the five senses:

  Sight _____

  Touch _____

  Hearing _____

  Smell _____

  Taste _____

- Keep your adult leaders encouraged with the awesome ideas you'll find in *Go Team! 101 Ideas to Energize Youth Ministry Volunteers* by Kurt Johnston and Katie Edwards (Group Publishing, Inc.).

Now What? Ideas

continued

- Take a trip to your local bookstore or library, and scan through a few books on marketing and management. Find some business insights that are transferable to youth ministry, and allow them to motivate you to increase customer service. Here are a few business-oriented books I've found to be very helpful:

Customer Satisfaction Is Worthless, Customer Loyalty Is Priceless by Jeffrey Gitomer

Fabled Service: Ordinary Acts, Extraordinary Outcomes by Betsy Sanders

Good to Great by Jim Collins

How to Win Friends and Influence People by Dale Carnegie

Keeping Good People by Roger E. Herman

Love 'Em or Lose 'Em by Beverly L. Kaye and Sharon Jordan-Evans

Pour Your Heart Into It by Howard Schultz

Service Magic by Ron Zemke and Chip Bell

The Spirit to Serve Marriott's Way by J.W. Marriott Jr. and Kathi Ann Brown

The Tipping Point by Malcolm Gladwell

_____

_____

_____

_____

_____

_____

_____

_____

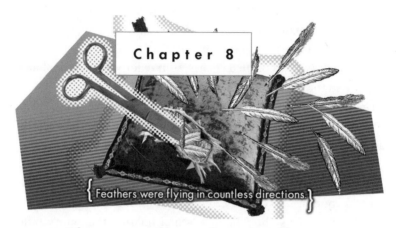

{ Feathers were flying in countless directions. }

The #1 Killer of Friendly Youth Ministries...and How to Take Aim

Ever done one of your counseling sessions on the top of your church roof with a feather pillow in your hands? I did. And reminiscing back on that crisp fall afternoon, I think Jesus was probably smiling. Let me explain the situation.

Early on in my youth ministry journey, I became convinced that the number one killer of a thriving youth group wasn't sex or drugs. The enemy I'd come to fear most was far sneakier in his approach. He hid behind pious smiles and mingled between quiet prayers and worship songs. He never forced his way into our group from the outside. Instead, he resided among us and even attended most every youth gathering held. Who was this number one killer of a friendly youth ministry? Gossip.

It was this conniving enemy I was confronting high atop our church sanctuary roof that chilly October afternoon. With pillow and scissors in hand, I had instructed two of the more popular girls in our youth group to follow me to the roof. They initially laughed at the strangeness of the request, yet they giddily climbed the outdoor ladder for three stories. When we arrived at our destination, we were slightly out of breath. We made small talk for a few minutes before we officially began our time together.

"OK, ladies," I said, "Would you be so kind as to take these scissors and cut open this feather pillow for me?" The girls glanced awkwardly at each other and then began cutting away. Feathers immediately started to fall out and were caught up by the wind. One of the girls quickly folded over the opening, in reaction to the obvious.

"No, that's OK," I coached them. "I'd like for you both to shake the pillow now so the feathers can fly all over."

Their faces, once filled with humor, were now serious. Perhaps they were beginning to realize that my inviting them to a session on the rooftop had some significance. Still with a puzzled look in their eyes, they began to shake the open pillow over the edge of the tall building. The fall wind left little options for the hundreds of feathers that fell out. Feathers were flying in countless directions, and within minutes, all of them had disappeared out of our sight. The girls stood holding the empty pillowcases, wondering what was next.

"Now ladies, I have just one more instruction," I continued. "Please leave this rooftop, and gather up all the feathers you turned loose in the wind." The girls just awkwardly gazed at me as though attempting to understand what they had just been asked to do.

"That's impossible!" one of the girls finally blurted out.

"It sure is," her friend chimed in. "We can't collect all those feathers, Jeanne. The wind has blown them to places we'll never even know."

"Exactly." I answered firmly. "And that is just what has happened to your gossip about Melinda. Your negative words about her have blown all over the youth group. She's pretty broken up, knowing she can't possibly chase down all the rumors and set the record straight. Do you ladies understand what I'm trying to say?"

Only the whisper of the fall wind broke the silence. The girls dropped their heads, not knowing how to answer. I had already tried on two earlier occasions to correct their "gift of gab," but without lasting success. My rooftop illustration had been my last-ditch effort to help the two high

"Often the negative impact of gossip is minimized as just part of the normal adolescent experience."

school ladies understand the serious impact of their gossip and backbiting. This time my point had been made.

Why the Serious Approach?

It has often amazed me how easily the enemy infiltrates our ranks through gossip and how casually we respond to his assaults. Over and over, Scripture reminds us that unity is an essential part of Christian community. Yet youth leaders often allow gossip and divisive talk to go unaddressed, causing painful wounds and sometimes irreversible divisions. Remember that Group Magazine survey I mentioned in Chapter 1? I continue to reference it because I want your entire approach to youth ministry to be permanently impacted by this simple revelation: 73 percent of all teenagers surveyed said their number one criteria for a youth ministry was "a welcoming atmosphere where you can be yourself." Coming in a close second, 70 percent of those responding said that their top desire in a youth ministry was "quality relationships with other teenagers."

Both of those essential ingredients are absolutely impossible to create and sustain if gossip takes center stage in the life of a youth ministry. Often the negative impact of gossip is minimized as just part of the normal adolescent experience. But since authentic friendship is one of youth ministry's most powerful drawing cards, I think the enemy delights in planting seeds of gossip and negative slander in almost every youth ministry. Sometimes it is pointed at students, and at other times, it is directed at the leadership team.

The book of Proverbs uses some vivid language to describe people of this nature. Outdated as King James language might seem, the wording gives us contemporary word pictures for gossip. Proverbs 25:23 calls it "backbiting" and Proverbs 26:20 uses "talebearing." The picture of someone sneaking up behind another person and literally taking a bite out of the back may be humorous. Yet it gives us a pretty accurate description of gossip. The term *talebearing* brings to mind images of Paul Revere's ride, but instead of a worthy message like, "The British are coming," the message is one of character assassination. Whatever the specifics of the situation, the impact of gossip is not to be overlooked.

Gossip is a serious issue. It shouldn't be overlooked or ignored. Left on its own, gossip can become a cancer spreading throughout your youth group. Let me share with you a few observations about gossip drawn from my years in youth ministry:

- Generally speaking, teenage girls tend to gossip much more frequently than guys. This isn't a slam against girls, and I know this isn't true in every case. However, I have found that adolescent girls are more prone to be gossips because of deep emotional issues that often create the problem.

- Gossip is often rooted in either jealousy or insecurity. If you as a leader understand the root of the problem, you'll be much more successful in dealing with it.

- Teenagers often learn to be gossips at home. Ever heard the old saying, "The apples don't fall too far from the tree"? That is painfully true when it comes to teenagers and their parents. Thus, many teenagers who have a tendency to talk negatively about others have grown up in homes where gossip is an everyday practice. And just because a family is Christian, doesn't necessarily lower the odds of it being a family of gossip and backbiting. Some of the most habitual gossips I have ever known have been Christians. Sadly, Christians have created the guise under which to share negative information about others without casting ourselves in a negative light. Why, of course we're not gossiping—we're just sharing prayer requests!

- People seem to believe that *true* information cannot be considered gossip. Many times when I've confronted a teenager about something they have said, their defensive reply is, "But it was the truth!" Yet whether something is true or untrue doesn't matter; Scripture instructs us to not gab about negative information about others. There are three acceptable responses to negative information about someone else.

Give a Glimpse of Gossip

"One time I was with a few girls and another leader from youth group. One of the teenagers began to gossip about one of their friends. Immediately I turned to the leader beside me and began to gossip about my best friend. The girls stopped talking and looked at me like, 'What are you doing?!' I turned to them and said, 'Obviously that wasn't true, but if you're shocked to hear me say something like that about one of my friends, you should think twice about what you're saying about *your* friend.'"

—Monica Neal, youth worker in Fort Smith, Arkansas

1) We may go directly to the person being talked about and share with them our concern,
2) We may keep our mouths totally closed and make it a matter of sincere prayer, or
3) We may take the information to a trusted spiritual leader who has the wisdom to orchestrate any needed follow-up action.

Unless a person is part of the scriptural answer to the situation, they do not need to be involved. The fact that the negative information is true does not erase the Bible's clear direction to us in this arena.

A More Subtle Verbal Weapon

Gossip isn't the only dangerous enemy. In fact, gossip has an ugly cousin who often tags along. This cousin can become second nature to us, and yet we don't even realize that our words have painful effects. It is so common in our culture that you'll probably be surprised I even consider it a threat to developing a thriving youth ministry. Who is this second verbal enemy? Sarcasm.

Today's youth culture so loves humor that sarcasm is often viewed as a youth ministry friend rather than a foe, yet this obsession with comedy often builds a "humor at any price" philosophy. Sarcasm is usually a measure of truth wrapped in barbing humor at someone else's expense. I've known many "cool" youth leaders who have become specialists at communicating with teenagers through sarcasm. Ironically, the students they feel the most connected to are often the ones who get the brunt of their verbal jabs. The youth leader, who doesn't realize what he or she is doing, thinks, "The student knows I'm only joking. I kid with him that way because I really like him." Yet Proverbs 26:18-19 describes this behavior in a less glamorous light: "Like a madman shooting firebrands or deadly arrows is a man who deceives his neighbor and says, 'I was only joking!'" Ouch!

Sarcasm is a challenging enemy because it is so applauded by today's media. It often becomes a form of male pride and takes its toll by making people feel awkward about themselves and off-balance in their environment. Because words of affirmation are awkward for people to verbalize, sarcasm becomes an alternative way to communicate friendship and warmth. My heart goes out most to youth leaders who have never been taught a better

> *"Like a madman shooting firebrands or deadly arrows is a man who deceives his neighbor and says, 'I was only joking!'"* —Proverbs 26:18-19

way to verbalize authentic affection. Sadly, some youth leaders function in the mind-set that sees sincere words of affirmation as a sign of weakness rather than strength.

I remember years ago saying to one of my favorite leaders, "Barry, you're amazing. But could you think about dropping the sarcasm from your humor?" He paused for a moment and then responded sincerely, "Jeanne, if I cut all the sarcasm out of my vocabulary, I'll probably be completely quiet for the next month!" Although Barry's honesty was rare, I don't think his problem was all that uncommon. Sarcasm comes pretty easy for most of us. I don't think it is wrong to poke fun at situations or circumstances, but I think we easily cross the line when our sarcasm is centered on another person. We don't intend to hurt them, yet time and time again our words cut like a knife.

It isn't always just the teenagers. As I train youth leaders around the nation, I repeatedly say to the crowds: "Youth leaders, please try to have the guts to drop the sarcasm when you joke around with your students. Train yourselves, as awkward as it might feel at first, to become a person who affirms others with your words. And if it takes sarcasm pointed at someone else to be funny, please be strong enough to drop the comedy. Though none of your teenagers will ever say it to you, they want your approval so much that they inwardly remember almost everything you say about them. You may know you're joking, but they don't."

Taking Aim at Gossip and Sarcasm

In short, if you want to create a youth ministry culture of authentic friendship and growth, both gossip and sarcasm will need to find the back door of your youth gathering. However, like many important concepts, this goal is much easier stated than accomplished. But don't worry—it can be done! Here are a few simple "how to's" for dealing with gossip and sarcasm. I promise you, the work you put in to making these ideas happen will be worth the results.

1. As with all significant changes, get your key influencers on your side.
Begin to create an epidemic of positive verbal change in your youth ministry by making a list (short or long) of influential students who you need to get on your team. (Paul Revere would be proud of you!)

Take each of these folks out for pizza or coffee, and make your appeal. Tell them you need their help in changing the culture of your youth group from one of gossip and sarcasm to one of warmth and encouragement. Don't be negative or sound too preachy in your comments, and be sure to ask for any suggestions they might have to offer.

Not too long ago I had to deal with a pocket of gossip that was traced back to three specific girls. I went to the three girls individually to discuss the problem with them. I made sure my tone of voice was loving and understanding so they wouldn't feel defensive. I told them I knew sometimes we all say things about others that are negative, and at times we find a little insecurity in ourselves that makes us talk about others behind their backs. I explained to each of them that I knew they didn't mean to purposefully hurt anyone, but their names had come up several times and one particular person had been quite hurt. I asked them if they'd be willing to help stop the pattern of gossip in the youth group.

Two of the three did get a little defensive, but I remained loving and direct. In those types of conversations, it's best to keep mentally saying, "Don't react; respond." Using "we" statements instead of "you" statements creates bridges of understanding that can make your efforts more effective.

As with the example of the three girls who were at the core of the gossip problem, sarcasm in your group can probably also be traced back to a handful of sharp, well-liked kids. Take time to approach these individuals, and ask them to help create a climate of fun that is encouraging, not caustic.

2. Create a youth meeting focused on gossip or sarcasm. You could even call the talk, "Lessons From a Feather Pillow"! If you are dealing with gossip, you might begin the evening by

Skip Sarcasm

"I have watched too many youth pastors do their best to fight off fears of being un-cool by using sarcasm with their students. This is never the way to connect with people. I've found that when you give respect to them, they give it back to you. It starts at the top."
—Brent Parsley, youth worker in Colorado Springs, Colorado

showing a video of yourself and another student on top of a roof holding a pillow. Re-enact my opening true story with your own fictional characters. After showing the video, begin your challenge with a feather pillow in hand. Consider having two or three students who have been hurt by gossip, share about how it affected them. You could also invite a student who is trying to break the gossip habit share about his or her struggle to change. (Make sure you coach students ahead of time so they are well prepared.) At the conclusion of the event, use a fan to blow the feathers all over the room. Ask your students to each retrieve one of the feathers. Then have them pray with the feathers in their hands, asking God to help them change.

If you're dealing primarily with sarcasm, the feather pillow night ideas may be easily adapted for your evening. Or, instead of focusing on the feather pillow object lesson, create an original drama depicting a few students being funny and sarcastic toward each other. End the drama by having one student do a monologue, saying something like, "Those guys sure are fun to hang out with, but sometimes I wonder if they really do think I'm a big loser. I mean, they say they're joking about me being a rotten basketball player. Man, if they only knew what a jerk I feel like after every Friday night game. It's all real funny, except for one thing. I'm the joke and right now, I'm not laughing."

3. If students don't change their ways, have the courage to confront them more seriously. The trip to the rooftop I took with those two girls was not the first time I had dealt with them about gossip. I had asked them to stop on two previous occasions. I had already explained the principle from Matthew 18:15 that instructs Christians to go directly to the person they have a problem with instead of talking about them behind their back, yet the girls' gossip continued. As I experienced with these students, there comes a point when loving confrontation needs to be firm and direct. Have the courage to confront students (or leaders) when necessary. Don't assume that by dedicating a youth group meeting to the topic, gossip and sarcasm will just go way; it won't. Because confrontation can feel so awkward, it's tempting to avoid it and instead just ignore the problem. Ask God to give you the courage to directly address the key offenders in your group. The long-term damage to the unity of your youth ministry will be greater than you think if you look the other way and pretend nothing is going on.

4. In extreme cases, you might need to ask a student to take time away from your youth group. Many youth leaders wonder about when—or if—it is acceptable to ask a student to leave the youth group. The problem may be gossip, sarcasm, cursing, alcohol abuse, or worse. Even though it is painful to do, after over three decades in youth ministry I've learned the incredible value of telling a student that he or she needs to stay clear of youth functions for one to three months. This extreme measure should only be taken when a student refuses to change his or her behavior and the conduct is a disruption to the entire group. When I've had to ask students to take a break from the group, it has usually been because they were repeatedly disruptive or disrespectful, but there have been a few times I've had to deal with gossiping or sarcastic kids in this manner.

Asking a student to leave and not attend youth functions is never easy. When I do so, I mentally remind myself of what I call, "The Inoculation Principle." When you go to the doctor to receive a vaccination, what does the doctor inject in your body? Ironically, it's often a form of the actual virus you're being inoculated against. You don't receive enough of it to give you the disease; instead, you are given just enough to make you immune to the real thing. In much the same way, we often unknowingly "inoculate" students *against* the thrill of a real relationship with Christ. How? We do this by allowing them to come to our youth meetings, cause problems, and never truly listen to the claims of Christ. Little by little, they build up an "immunity" to the Lord by getting used to the experience of the group without taking the Gospel message seriously. It would have been far better for them and those around them if they had stayed home until they could attend the group within the basic behavioral guidelines.

I can hear sincere mercy-driven readers saying, "Didn't Jesus leave the ninety-nine sheep in the fold to go after the one? Wouldn't kicking a kid out be violating this principle?" My answer to this is simple: Leaving the ninety-nine for the one is not the same as *sacrificing* the ninety-nine for the one. Unfortunately, youth leaders often sacrifice the well-being of the

> **"Leaving the ninety-nine for the one is not the same as sacrificing the ninety-nine for the one."**

group as a whole because we lack the courage to confront the one or two students who are creating the problem.

Create a Positive Atmosphere of Affirmation and Encouragement

I often remind our youth leadership team, "Don't pull the weeds without planting the flowers." The best way to remove negative behavior is to replace it with something positive. One of the most powerful ways to overcome gossip and sarcasm is to focus on creating a positive culture of verbal affirmation and encouragement. Remember the frog-kissing story in Chapter 1? Jesus used encouragement to help "kiss the frog" out of Simon and bring forth the rock-like character of the true Peter. But I bet if we had known Simon in his pre-Jesus days, we might have found him to be a humorous and sarcastic guy. He probably was a fun person to be around and quickly rose to leadership, but I'm sure there were a few disciples who sat on the end of his verbal barbs. Jesus might have had to "pull some weeds" during private conversations with Peter (I can just hear Jesus saying, "Pete, you can't keep dogging on Andrew no matter how funny your cracks about his constipated camel are!"). Yet Jesus didn't just tell his followers what *not* to do. He always clearly outlined the positive alternative he wanted them to use to replace the negative. Creating an atmosphere of positive words and encouragement is one of the best flower-planting exercises you can do in youth ministry, especially when working to put an end to sarcasm and gossip.

Some Honest Words to Every Leader

Remember the profound leadership principle, "We teach what we know, but we reproduce who we are"? That principle could not be more valid than in the area of creating an affirming, encouraging culture in youth ministry. To put it bluntly: Your youth ministry will gradually begin to mirror your own conversation style. With that in mind, it is absolutely imperative as a leader that you train your mind to search for positive things about everyone you meet. Ralph Waldo Emerson once wrote, "Each [man] is incomparably superior to his companion in some faculty." We should emulate this mind-set, considering others better than ourselves and seeking to find positive things to say about each person we meet.

"Be hearty in your approbation and lavish in your praise." —Dale Carnegie

In the 1930s, Dale Carnegie gave up his career as a salesman to design and teach a course about relating well with others. He taught the class at a YMCA in New York City, and it became very successful and widely attended. One night a publisher attended his class and persuaded Carnegie to put his course materials into a book. That book, titled *How to Win Friends and Influence People,* sold like wildfire and was on the New York Times Best-Seller List for ten years. It's still a big seller today.

Being the wise youth leader you are, I'm sure you are asking the same question I once asked: What's the bottom line of Dale Carnegie's human relationship theories? Carnegie summed it all up in this principle: "Be hearty in your approbation and lavish in your praise." In short, Dale Carnegie taught that successful leaders train themselves to be individuals who search for honest, positive things they can communicate to others. That truth is quite applicable to youth ministry. Again, I'm not saying never to correct or admonish. I just want to emphasize that whatever behaviors you reward with praise and encouragement will get repeated. So if you want a positive culture of affirmation and fun in the midst of a sarcastic, cutting society, it all begins with *you.*

As we close, let me share with you a few words from a former U.S. president: "This is a pain I mostly hide...and even now I feel inside the hunger for his outstretched hand, a man's embrace to take me in, the need for just a word of praise." President Jimmy Carter's words are no different than what any average teenager feels. That same craving for acceptance and praise is alive in every teenager God places on your path. When Christ's love flows from you to connect with that craving, the life-impacting results will be astonishing.

I couldn't ask to be remembered for anything greater than to have lavished love and encouragement on the students I work with. I hope to have planted enough flowers that when teenagers remember me, they'll say, "She believed in me, she saw the best in me, and she said it."

Now What? Ideas

Use these ideas to put the principles
in this chapter into action:

- Study Proverbs and compile a list of verses that apply to gossip, put-downs, and sarcasm. Use the list in your daily time with God, asking him to change your own habits of gossip or sarcasm. Consider sharing some Scriptures with students who need to read biblical principles on this subject.

- Eat something sweet. As you do, pray that God will give you sweet words of affirmation for the students in your group.

- Consider hosting a "feather pillow" night demonstrating the effects of gossip.

- Listen to some sarcastic phrases you hear every day or on television or even among your group. Write them down, and then use them in a drama students can perform. In all seriousness, act as if what was said was meant literally, making the teenagers step back and realize that it's not always funny. Use the drama to start a discussion about the impact words have on us.

- Ask several of the students in your group to share honestly how sarcastic remarks affect them.

- Prayerfully consider which students you might need to pull aside privately to discuss gossiping or sarcastic habits. Write down their names, and set up times to take them out for coffee or pizza to discuss the issue.

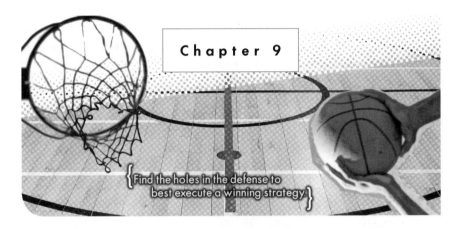

{Find the holes in the defense to best execute a winning strategy}

Creating a Cosby Family Feeling in an Osbourne Family World

Remember the old sitcom with the Huxtables—Cliff, Clair, Sondra, Denise, Theo, Vanessa, and Rudy? At the height of *The Cosby Show's* success, they were often referred to as "America's favorite family." If you get a chance to watch some of the old reruns, you'll see that the Cosby family still represents a lot of what young people today crave. The show depicts a family that laughs together, cries together, fights together, and communicates honestly with each other.

In contrast, more recent years have brought us a quite different famous TV family: the Osbournes. If you ever watched this reality show, you know it is quite an experience, complete with a high number of "bleeps" that cover up questionable language about every thirty seconds. Just the other night I spotted the show while channel-surfing my way to CNN. In that particular episode, the family members were loudly yelling at each other about everything from weekend plans to opinions on a current movie. It was a sharp contrast from *The Cosby Show* of the '80s.

Many teenagers today live in broken homes, so it is little wonder that youth ministries that purposefully cultivate a sense of belonging and family are much more effective than typical detached youth groups. Let me wrap up this book with a few more suggestions for how you can increase the "Cosby-factor" in your youth ministry. Be warned: The "Osbourne-factor" will always grow without effort among your students, simply due to our self-centered human nature. But the "Cosby-factor" doesn't grow by itself. It takes strategic work and cultivation on your part.

Rev Up the Friendship Factor With a Point Guard Ministry

I suppose everyone who has ever written a book reaches moments in their writing where they want to say to the reader, "Please, read this carefully. It's a small idea that can make a big difference if you implement it." Candidly, that is exactly how I feel about setting up a Point Guard ministry in your weekly youth meetings. So grab your highlighter, and make sure the next couple of paragraphs get your full attention because they could make a big difference in the friendship factor of your youth ministry. This system will help your group grow both spiritually and numerically.

The term *point guard* in basketball refers to the key player on the offense who helps to create the plays in the game. We define the word for our group as:

> **Point Guard** (point) (gard) n. the person who finds the holes in the defense to best execute a winning strategy.

The implications of this term in youth ministry are huge. I created this program when I needed a grassroots leadership plan—one that would take an entry-level degree of ability, commitment, and spiritual maturity. Point Guard is a simple system of instituting row hosts and hostesses in your weekly youth meeting. These individuals can be students, adults, or a combination of both. You just need to map out the area where your youth group meets each week in order to determine the specific rows, chairs, or couches you want each of your Point Guard leaders to be responsible for. Ask these individuals to "own" whoever sits in those seats each week. The students who sit in their row may vary from week to week, but you'll find that many of the same students will develop relationships with those they sit by and will return to the same seating area each week. We all know the feeling, whether our group has nine students or nine hundred, of wanting everyone to feel authentically connected with, both spiritually and relationally. A Point Guard ministry provides a simple system whereby this can occur on a consistent basis.

Students on your Point Guard team should do the following:

- Show up early to meetings and warmly welcome everyone who sits in their assigned area.

- Look carefully for people who might be guests, welcome them, and invite them to sit in their area.

- Introduce each guest to at least one other student in the group.

- Kindly make sure the students in their area aren't being disruptive during the youth meeting.

- Take a few minutes once a month to give small gifts to everybody in their area. The gifts should always cost less than one dollar, such as pieces of gum or goofy stickers. (We've made this a fun tradition by celebrating "Christmas" every month. We crank up fun Christmas music and allow the Point Guard people to go down their rows, handing out gifts. Everyone loves getting gifts, and this is an easy way to make new visitors feel like a part of your youth family. Just make sure you do it the same time each month, and you might want to call your leaders ahead to remind them. I usually keep back-up gifts at the church, just in case someone forgets.)

- *Own* the individuals that sit in their area by treating them as good friends and going out of their way to make all of them feel welcomed.

- Pray before and during the youth meeting that the people who sit in their area will have an authentic encounter with Jesus.

- Talk with guests after the meeting, and invite them to return the next week.

- Make a mental note of people who didn't show up on a particular week, and make an effort to call them and see how they're doing.

- Attend fun Point Guard team meetings about every six weeks.

As you form a Point Guard team, think of it as a way to get students who may not be spiritual superstars involved in ministry. It is an exceptional launching pad for training new leaders in your youth group and helps students feel a sense of ownership as they work together to form a sense of true community in your youth ministry.

Eat Together

One of the best ways to deepen friendships and build a family atmosphere is by eating together. It is no accident that so many important teachings occurred between Jesus and his friends while they were dining together. Have you ever noticed how tough it is to have dinner with an enemy and remain enemies? If you want to cultivate the "Cosby-factor" in a generation of "Osbourne-like families," plan some times when all or part of your group eats together.

This can be anything from stopping together at the "Golden Arches" on the way home from a trip, or hosting a picnic on the Fourth of July. Every three months, I invite all of my adult leaders to my home for a "pitch-in" lunch after church because I know the magic that occurs when we all eat together. Whatever your particular together-meals are, never underestimate the significance of eating together to create great memories and deepen relationships.

Play Together

Every Cosby-family youth ministry knows the importance of not only *praying* together, but also *playing* together. One way we've done this is by hosting an annual flag football tournament in the fall that we've called "The Pumpkin Bowl." We've done it for years, and it not only facilitates fun, but it also builds tradition. Flag football turned out to be the easiest way to get all of our students and their friends involved in one huge event, but you could choose from a variety of other sports such as Wiffle ball, volleyball, and 3-on-3 basketball tournaments. Divide up teams, being careful to spread out the athletes in your group so there isn't an unbeatable team. Make it very clear that the goal to have fun together is a much bigger deal than the goal to win.

The first time we hosted a Pumpkin Bowl, it took some effort to get the teams excited and into the games. But as the years went by, teams began creating their own T-shirts, making their own cheers, and having team members dress up as cheerleaders and mascots. To help the sights and smells add to the excitement, we have parents run concession stands (with

"Never underestimate the significance of eating together to create great memories and deepen relationships."

hot dogs, hot chocolate, chips, and other snacks) and play loud up-tempo Christian music.

By the time the day is over, everyone is exhausted, exhilarated, and closer. During the months that follow, you will hear the students repeatedly reference the fun they had that day. Suddenly, through a sense of teamwork and unavoidable victories or defeats, the teenagers have shared memories that will bring them laughter and a sense of belonging for the rest of their lives.

Fun events like this are also an opportunity to reach out to non-Christian students. We've encouraged Pumpkin Bowl players to attend our next youth group meeting to watch a video of highlights from the games. Year after year, we have seen individuals come to faith in Christ at the youth meeting following the Pumpkin Bowl. I smile as I recall the names of amazing young athletes who came to faith through this avenue of outreach. One student recently told me, "I showed up at Oxygen just to see the highlight video and pick up my winner's sweatshirt. But I left knowing Christ in a real way. The more I watch things around here, the more I'm convinced that Oxygen is a finely-tuned conspiracy!" And you know what? I think that high school guy was right. A finely tuned conspiracy—what a great compliment!

Retreats, Road Trips, Overnighters

I'm about to make a true confession: At this point in my life as a youth pastor, my idea of fun is getting to sleep in my own bed at night—and at a decent hour! How about you? However,

Eight Is Enough

"So many teenagers need a sense of family, and it's hard for youth pastors to get close to their kids on a deeper level. We started doing what we called, "Dinner for Eight." Every month, we had eight teenagers over for a big family-style dinner, by invitation only. It was an awesome way for us to get to know them and them to get to know each other. After three or four months, we'd been able to spend quality time with all of our kids, and it began building a true sense of family."
—Matt Nash, youth worker in Robinson, Illinois

wise youth leaders know the importance of sacrificing that convenience occasionally to gain the closeness that can only be obtained through a road trip, retreat, or weekend together with students.

When we first started Oxygen, we hosted a lock-in at the church facility because finances made any other kind of trip difficult for our students. If you have ever hosted a lock-in for your students, you are undoubtedly wondering why I would put myself through this type of self-inflicted torture! Let's be honest: We should host support groups for youth leaders who have survived a junior high or high school lock-in! For those of us who have, we always tell ourselves we'll never do it again. As a woman in my fifties, it seems crazy to stay up all night with totally wild kids. But the simple truth is that trips and overnights together significantly increase the Cosby-factor in any youth group.

Road trips can be as simple as driving an hour together to spend a Saturday at an amusement park. After all, taking the church bus always increases everyone's faith! Or you could go camping together for a weekend. Ready-made events, like youth conferences or conventions held by your particular denomination are great if you're not ready to host your own. Choose something, get organized, and then enlist as many teenagers as you possibly can. You'll wind up with great memories and changed hearts.

Road trips are certainly fun, but through the years some of my greatest memories have come through our weekend retreats. Putting on your own retreat requires more work, more time, and more money. But hosting something that is fun and intensely spiritual for your own kids has monumental rewards.

Everywhere I've been privileged to have a youth group, we've done an annual fall retreat. We arrive at a campground on Friday evening and return Sunday afternoon. During the Friday and Saturday evening meetings, the students perform full-length dramas. Small-group discussion times are held on Saturday morning and afternoon and are centered around the

Hosting even just one overnight or all-day activity will begin to change the dynamics from a mere 'youth group' to a true 'youth family.'

spiritual message of the dramas. These weekends have proven to be our most significant way to build closeness in our youth ministry.

The simple point is that something almost magical happens when you spend longer blocks of time together with the students in your group. Like me, you might secretly dread trips, retreats, conventions, or all night lock-ins because of the stress and responsibility it entails. Yet, if the only time your group is together is your midweek youth group meeting, no matter how hard you try, you'll be unable to establish the sense of unity you're aiming for. Hosting even just one overnight or all-day activity will begin to change the dynamics from a mere "youth group" to a true "youth family."

Establish Traditions

I've often heard that good parents know how to give their children both roots and wings. In like manner, I think great youth leaders do the same for their youth ministries. One of the best ways to create a sense of roots among your teenagers is by establishing some traditions that become part of the DNA of your ministry. Here are a few traditions we've established— as you read, they may spark some new ideas of your own.

- We host a traditional Thanksgiving meal for the students who are seniors in high school. They meet at my home around 9:30 p.m. the Wednesday night before Thanksgiving right after our youth group meeting. I make the turkey, and the kids bring the rest of the food. It's always a great night of laughter and hanging out together.

- Around graduation, all of the seniors are invited back over to our home for "Midnight Communion." It's held late on a Friday night, and we spend the first fifteen to twenty minutes going around and writing a response to "What I most appreciate about you is…" on each others' backs. Then we play soft Christian music while we all take communion together and then pray for each other. Afterward the teenagers read the encouragements on their sheets of paper. Then we often go out for a 3 a.m. breakfast and wind up at someone's house swimming or watching movies until the sun comes up.

- We hold "Mud Olympics" in which we dig a massive hole in a large field near the church and fill it with water. We play tug of war, volleyball, and other games in the middle of the mud field. At the end of the day, the local firemen come out to hose everyone off. The memories (not to mention the pictures) are hysterical!

• One of my favorite traditions is among the men and women who I train for full-time youth ministry whom I fondly refer to as my interns. They are each given a ring with an inscription in Hebrew on it. Though the cost of this gesture is minimal, the impact of the "ring ceremony" and tradition it creates is monumental. To this day, I've had countless interns, some married and with children and full-time ministries, call and say, "I lost my ring. Can you order me a new one?" Why is it such a big deal to them? Because we made it special; and to teenagers as well as adults, traditions matter.

Another Family That Understood the Cosby-Factor

Long ago, I heard a story about a family in the Holocaust. Granted, they never made a television program like *The Cosby Show*, but they understood the importance of roots and wings. Their story gives us a great picture of the anchoring worth of family in a world of Osbourne-like homes.

> There were four people in the Stern family who were placed in a Nazi concentration camp—a father, mother, and two sons. During the day they were separated for their work assignments, but the mood was the most tense when they returned to the dimly lit bunker where they all stayed late each evening. What was the cause for the tenseness? The youngest son had weakened legs, and the family knew the Nazis would not tolerate his lack of productivity indefinitely. They had already known several other prisoners who were sent to the ovens to be exterminated. Each night they feared he would not return to the bunker alive.
>
> One evening Mr. Stern returned to the dark bunker and could not find the rest of his family. He became frantic. At last, he spotted the older son huddled in the back corner, weeping. "What's wrong?" he asked.
>
> Struggling to speak, the boy said, "This morning, after you left the bunker, they came for him. They told him they were going to take him to another place to live."

"But what about Mother?" the dad asked emotionally. "Where is Mother?"

Shaking, the boy cried, "When the men came for him, Father, he was very afraid. He began to weep and beg momma to help him."

"Yes," said the father. "I still do not understand."

"Well," David sobbed. "Momma wrapped her arms around him and said, 'I'll take care of you.' The last thing I heard her whisper was, 'You don't need to cry, darling. Wherever they take you, momma will go with you. Momma will hold you very, very close.' And they took them both away."

That, my friend, is the essence of what a thriving, effective youth ministry should be in our hurting world. Whether it's through midnight communion or Pumpkin Bowl hysteria, today's youth culture needs to feel they have Christian friends and leaders who will go through the tough times in life with them. In a world of Osbournes, they need their youth group to feel more like the Cosby family.

Concluding Thoughts

I pray you've gleaned some ideas and practical suggestions on how to grow your own youth ministry. From following up on visitors (Chapter 4), to enhancing the time you spend with teenagers by creating a more welcoming environment (Chapter 3), to creating an atmosphere free of gossip and sarcasm (Chapter 8), I hope you can begin to implement these ideas among the youth in your church. May you be encouraged and challenged to begin frog-kissing some warty teenagers that God's brought into your own life (Chapter 1). Please make sure in your efforts to grow numerically you remember that CEO of Starbucks' words "people are not a line item" (Chapter 7). Help your kids live their teenage years in a community in which they feel welcomed and enjoy the benefits from reaching out to others and

> ### A Family Christmas Card
>
> "We found an opportune moment to take a large group photo and later that year we had it turned into a greeting card. We could surprise everyone with a Christmas card with their picture on it, or use it as a way to invite kids back who happened to be in the picture but hadn't been around in a while."
>
> —Monica Neal, youth worker in Fort Smith, Arkansas

putting to rest "Mr. Clique" (Chapter 5). You'll see exciting results as you pull leaders and teenagers up-close to you and invest in them, one person at a time (Chapter 2). Above all, live out your life as a youth worker so that through the love of Christ, your teenagers know that no matter how hot their circumstances may get, you will go through them with them. As part of the family, Jesus' love through you will hold them very, very close. And you, my friend, will experience first-hand a thriving youth group.

> **"Above all, live out your life as a youth worker so that through the love of Christ, your teenagers know that no matter how hot their circumstances may get, you will go through them with them."**

Now What? Ideas

Use these ideas to put the principles
in this chapter into action:

- Brainstorm a creative youth meeting that is focused on creating a sense of family (such as chocolate cookie night).

- Think of your favorite family tradition growing up. Journal about it using these questions: What was meaningful about it? Why do you remember it so well? How can you replicate that feeling in your youth ministry?

- Plan a weekend retreat for your group. Need ideas? Check out *Go Deeper Retreats* (Group Publishing, Inc.).

- Make a list of a few specific lines or phrases you could use in your youth ministry that would enhance an atmosphere of "family."

- Consciously determine to begin occasionally using these phrases in your talks.

- Flip back through this book, and put bookmarks in the chapters that seem most applicable to your group. Commit to take the "Now What?" steps highlighted in those chapters.

_____

_____

_____

_____

_____

_____

_____

_____

_____